DESOLATE HEIGHTS

RECLAIMING LIFE FROM ADDICTION, ISOLATION, AND EMOTIONAL INSTABILITY

A. H. SHACKLEFORD

LUCIDBOOKS

Desolate Heights
Reclaiming Life from Addiction, Isolation, and Emotional Instability

Copyright © 2018 by A.H. Shackleford

Published by Lucid Books in Houston, TX
www.LucidBooksPublishing.com

ISBN-10: 1-63296-236-5
ISBN-13: 978-1-63296-236-2
eISBN-10: 1-63296-237-3
eISBN-13: 978-1-63296-237-9

Special Sales: Most Lucid Books titles are available in special quantity discounts. Custom imprinting or excerpting can also be done to fit special needs. Contact Lucid Books at Info@LucidBooksPublishing.com.

Table of Contents

Disclaimer

In this book, I discuss specific actions, behaviors, and choices that were unhealthy for me. I make no moral judgments about specific preferences or points of view regarding sexuality. It is not my intention to condone, question, or chastise. The choices I made were wrong for me personally. This book is not intended to be a commentary or perspective on human sexuality in any manner. It largely isn't about sex at all. It is about healing—living the life you were intended to live—not allowing shame, wounds, lies, idols, and ultimately addiction to sabotage your success.

This book is also not about pushing a specific religious agenda. My faith is a central theme in my journey, and you will see that play out in the pages that follow. But do not allow differences in theology to trip you up or cause you to question the core principles addressed here. I'm not a biblical scholar. The scriptures I share and my interpretations of them are a combination of my experiences, my pursuit of God, and the teachings of individuals I admire. I have my beliefs. You have yours. Please do not allow those differences to distract you from the story I have to share.

Preface

My first memory is from when I was four years old. I was sitting in front of a large window in a small, red rocking chair as my mom changed the sheets on my bed. The sun was shining through, and its rays propped up flecks of dust, creating the illusion that beams were piercing the morning air.

My second memory is of my cousin when both of us were five years old. I was lying on the bed. The old soap opera *General Hospital* played on the television in the background. My pants were pulled down and his mouth was on my penis as he taught me a game called "Hospital."

I set out to write a very different book. The first version of this manuscript was a spiritual how-to, but as I started writing, I realized I was not in a state to lead others closer to God. Instead, I chose to tell my story and how I worked to overcome unmet needs, unresolved trauma, and untapped emotions, and how I fully recovered from a 30-year journey into isolation and addiction. Many of the truths I set out to share are still woven throughout, but I wanted to open myself up to being frighteningly transparent on these pages. I've discovered that the very same things preventing me from walking with God, the same things crippling me from really walking at all, are fairly common struggles a lot of people face.

I learned that saying it all out loud and talking about the road I took, the mistakes I made, the time I burned, and the lies I accepted—all of this would help others much more than trying to be authoritative and act as if I had everything figured out.

I had to set this book aside several times. My wounds, my insecurities, and my shame forced me to. There were days when I was on fire to finish it, convinced it could make a big difference in the world. There were days when the voices in my head told me I had nothing of value to add to the conversation, that smarter people had already touched on anything I'd be able to share, that I should just quit, that it was just another dream that would end in disappointment. There were days when the voices told me I was only writing a book to draw attention to myself, to convince myself I was okay, that I had value, and that I was special. There were days when the voices told me that my wounds weren't tragic enough and my experiences weren't troubling enough to merit a work like this. There were days when the voices said I wasn't a good enough writer and I probably would never get around to finishing it anyway, so why was I wasting my time when I could be more productive?

But the last time I almost quit, God spoke directly to me. I was in Chattanooga on a two-week separation from my wife. After months of feeling stuck and not being able to move forward in reconciling our relationship, she decided she needed some space. I obliged and booked myself at an Airbnb rental for a few weeks, agreeing that we'd have no contact while I was gone. It was hard.

One night, after trying to stay balanced, trying to write, trying to be productive with my time, I broke down. It was a Saturday night. I had passed a church earlier in the day that offered Saturday night services, so I decided to go to God's house for guidance. I missed my family and felt uninspired to continue writing the book. It just didn't seem to be a priority for me any longer. It just wasn't going to work out. No one in my life wanted me to write the book, anyway. No one.

The pastor that night preached on Acts. He focused on Luke, the author of Acts, and the fact that Acts was Luke's second book (the Gospel of Luke was his first). The pastor talked about Luke's motivation for writing his Gospel. In the first lines of the book, Luke noted that all of his accounts had already been widely written about, but he thought it was a good idea to write them down again for the guy he was writing to. He was obeying the call of God to do something that had already been done, something that seemed like a redundant, ordinary thing to do. The pastor went on to talk about how Luke's second work—Acts—couldn't have happened without his first writing. If he hadn't finished the first task God had given him, he wouldn't have had the opportunity to complete the second.

I felt God hovering as this man preached. I felt like spotlights were squarely shining on me. God didn't care if a story like mine had been written before. He didn't care if I felt like I could do it justice. He didn't care if I thought the story could actually make a difference. He didn't care if everyone else in my life thought it was a bad idea. He only cared that I was obedient and finished it so He could use it and give me something else to do. Who knows what that future work might be.

So I finished it (obviously, you're reading it right now). In doing so, I've realized how long God has been preparing me for this work. Unknowingly, I've spent decades conducting research, gathering experiences, learning hard lessons, and having insights shared with me in various forms, all for the purpose of this book. I've carried an undeniable desire deep within me to publish a book, ever since high school. But I never had the clarity of purpose, never the ability to complete any of the other 20 books I've started. Only this one (for now).

The last thing I will say about this book is really important. It's the whole point of it. A counselor once told me I didn't need to be defined by my past. I didn't need to absorb a specific label. I didn't need to be a martyr. I could still help others and be of service. My story, he said, was to be shared with "safe people." But I think he was wrong.

In a world where we take everything at Facebook value, it's easy to believe you are the only one with a problem, the only one struggling, the only one who doesn't have it all together. The truth is, most of us are limping around with deep wounds and dying for someone else to notice and help us. Too often, those who take ownership of a problem in their lives do so as quietly as possible. They don't want to add embarrassment. They don't want to let anyone down. They don't want to risk their reputation and relationships, so they hide it. Whether they are healing or hurting, getting better or getting worse, they hide it. Even when they are on the other side, they are coached to not be vulnerable with people who might not be safe.

I want to take things back to the third grade. Remember when you couldn't get full credit for a math answer unless you "showed your work"? That's what this book is—showing my work, letting you in on the secret that everyone has secrets. You aren't alone. You aren't even the minority. The more people who will stand up, be vulnerable, and share their stories, the more our society can actually start healing some of its deepest wounds collectively and individually. Then we can stamp out the stigmas stuck to everything from addiction and abuse to anxiety and depression. We can break through the isolation that separates us from one another and from our higher power.

So, you aren't quite right? You've made mistakes? You've been hurt? You've hurt others? You have secrets that feel too dark to ever share? You have shame? You want more from life and sometimes wonder if you deserve it?

That's the same backdrop for the story I'm about to tell you.

Each day I risk my life.
I put everything on the line.
I face danger without flinching.
I battle the enemy.
I do what must be done.
I do it over and over again.
I persevere. I don't quit.
I fight. I scratch. I claw.
And somehow, I live to see the sun rise again.
At least one more time.
I am not a hero.
Or a solider.
I'm an addict.

Introduction

Everyone looks at the addict and thinks, "Poor thing," or "Good for them for getting help." But addicts have a secret over everyone else. We know our enemy, and we are actively engaged in the fight. So don't have pity on us. Instead, look in the mirror and ask yourself, *What about me?*

A friend once told me addicts are the lucky ones. He was specifically referring to individuals undergoing some form of recovery. Such people, he said, get to see God in all His glory. They live life in surrender to Him and experience daily miracles. They are flawed for sure. But they are alive, and if they are diligent in giving their addictions to God, they do amazing things in His name. I agree. The addicts (those in active recovery) that I've encountered over the last few years are the most genuine, generous, grace-filled people walking the face of the earth. They are fallen angels who had to go through hell to find heaven and reclaim their wings.

Here's the big, dirty secret, though. We are all addicted to something. In *Breathing Under Water*, Richard Rohr suggests that addiction is simply a "modern name and honest description for what the biblical tradition called 'sin,' and medieval Christians called 'passions' or 'attachments.'"[1]

My intention is not to trivialize addiction in any way. I am also not trying to absolve us from accountability for the choices we make

1

in life by suggesting we are powerless to take different paths. But here's the thing. As a society, our armor is too often self-medication. We all have coping mechanisms. We all have vices. Some of us use things that are easy to identify such as alcohol, drugs, sex, or gambling. Some of us are caught up in codependency, trapped in obsessive thinking, paralyzed by anxiety, caged by relentless depression, suffering in quiet desperation, or enslaved to negative self-limiting beliefs. We drink, we eat, we rage, we spend, we envy. The bottom line is that everyone is an addict in one way or another, to one degree or another. And we all medicate in different ways. Many of them are not healthy responses.

Most people don't know who or what they are even fighting. Some don't know they have wandered into the ring. They just keep taking blows to the face, kicks to the mid-section, bruises and bumps and broken bones and bloody noses. And they don't feel a thing.

So I say to you…Wake up! It's easier than you think to wander through life numb, safe, and unfeeling. We are in real danger of looking up at the end of the ride and saying, "I missed the whole thing," jumping from one worry to the next, one crisis to the next, one want to the next, one sin to the next. Instant gratification. Self-centered fear. We just push the pain down. We go dark. We close our eyes and picture something, anything else.

For years, God tried to wake me up from my self-medication through all the traditional approaches. He poked my conscience. He placed men in my life who were wrestling with the same issues. He delivered daily visions during quiet time that might as well have been billboards on the side of the road. He allowed anxiety to build and my marriage to be strained under the weight of secrets. He permitted narrow escapes from negative consequences, providing multiple chances for me to shake myself out of the trance I was in. He got louder and louder. I still didn't answer.

But then He rocked me to consciousness.

Introduction

It was the quiet click of the handcuffs tightening around my wrists. It was the quiet click of the camera and my picture on the evening news and in the morning paper. But it might as well have been a freight train through my bedroom. I woke up for the first time—well, maybe ever. And luckily, it wasn't too late.

I don't know where you are today as you read my story or how far you or someone you love has gone. Maybe you're in an early stage of the struggle, and this book can serve as a dose of prevention. Or maybe you're in up to your neck and see no way out, and this book can serve as a dose of hope. Either way, as they say in recovery, I'm glad you're here.

*"Something's wrong when you regret
things that haven't happened yet."*
—"1940," The Submarines

CHAPTER 1

Day of the Arrest

The street was strangely still. I sat in my car, gripping the wheel. Birds on a telephone wire ahead were the only sign of life. They flitted about with no sound. The street sat quietly. Coldly. The air wasn't breathing. The rusted chain link, the cracked sidewalks, a few cars parked with no owners in sight. No life. A worn sign for a hipster coffee shop hung just to the left of an abandoned lot. It was old South meets urban living and the only sign of life within this barren swath of city.

There at the steering wheel, my hands firmly attached, my forehead pressing into the wheel, I was filled with regret for all I had already done, and even more for what I was about to do. I raised my head, my eyes staring off into the distance. The weight of my decisions pressed down on my chest with great force, making it hard to catch my breath.

A few minutes later, all eyes raised to watch me as I entered the coffee shop, ordered my food, and awkwardly shuffled to a table across the room. I wasn't surprised that I didn't fit in there. I never felt comfortable anywhere. I crunched into a BLT sandwich: crispy, salty bacon; a juicy, ripe tomato; perfectly green leaves of lettuce. My mouth watered as the meal quenched my hunger, and for just a moment, I wasn't really thinking about anything else.

The guy at the table next to me was wrestling with his own demons. The smell of alcohol coming from his pores was strong. He didn't appear to be a musician and was a bit too old for the club scene. My best guess was that he was just returning from a business trip where the drinks were flowing, and he had rolled right into an early morning flight home. He was the only person in the coffee shop who looked more out of place than I did. And almost as miserable.

I rushed through my sandwich and completed an obligatory networking meeting with the woman I had come to talk with. Listening to her passion for the nonprofit organization she had founded, I tried not to yawn. I feebly attempted to get the thoughts out of my head. I would have much preferred to listen intently and be stirred with emotion by this courageous woman. Instead, I was fantasizing about what was going to happen next. I wanted it to happen. Needed it to happen. And most definitely, absolutely, dreaded it happening. Regretted that it was going to happen. All at the same time.

At the close of our meeting, I hurriedly packed my workbag, dumped my empty cup and plate, and bolted for the door, my spare phone queued up and ready to make the call.

She answered. Adrenaline kicked in as I scheduled the appointment and received directions. It was a short drive down the interstate, a quick left, and then an immediate right. And I was there. I parked my car and walked intently through the front door of the hotel, avoiding eye contact with staff members and other guests. I slipped into the elevator, punched the third floor, and waited anxiously, hoping for the doors to close before anyone else could enter.

As I exited onto the third floor, a pit formed in my stomach. My intuition told me something just wasn't right—not that anything was right about this entire experience. But even in the context of what I was doing, something really wasn't right. I walked down the hall, pressing through the warning signs. This was merely the latest in a string of actions that were inherently risky. I was no longer making decisions in any rational manner. In fact, it was like it wasn't even a decision I had the power to make in that moment. I felt compelled to do it.

The room number she provided was at the very end. My steps quickened the closer I got to the door of Room 302, and I started to sweat, a nervous sweat even more intense than usual.

To my left, there was a room with the safety lock folded outward and the door slightly cracked. That seemed odd. Maybe it was just the cleaning crew propping it open. But as I approached her door, my intuition kicked in even harder—my gut told me to run. So I did. I took a hard left and bounded down a flight of stairs. I hit the second floor, exited into the hallway and hurried down the length of the building in the opposite direction of her room.

But as I reached the opposite stairwell, I did something I still can't explain. Instead of going down, I went back up to the third floor.

Everything in my body was sending alerts. Danger! Warning! Turn around! But for some reason, I couldn't. I shook all of it off. *Paranoia*, I told myself, *that's all you're feeling.*

Reaching her door, I almost had to pick up my right fist and force it to knock. She answered. She wasn't terribly attractive and definitely looked nothing like the picture from her ad. But I wasn't there to meet a beauty queen. She would do. I needed a fix.

She instructed me to place my donation on the dresser and get comfortable while she used the restroom. I set the money in plain sight as I was asked to do and sat on the edge of the bed. I loosened the laces on my left shoe and slid it off my foot. As I moved to my right foot, the door to the room flew open. As soon as it budged, I knew who was there.

A quartet of officers poured into the room. They handcuffed me, walked me across the hall to the room I had noticed earlier, and sat me on the couch next to the window. After reading me my rights, they told me I was under arrest for soliciting prostitution and then peppered me with questions. I pleaded with them. I promised I was just looking for a massage and that I wasn't trying to engage in illegal activity.

But they continued to press me. The lead questioner fully intended to intimidate me, and it was working. He was slightly older than me, tall with broad shoulders, a deep voice, and piercing eyes. A second officer stood to his left, a gangly young man who could barely fill out his uniform and appeared to be fresh out of the academy. He was staring down at me with a twisted lip and a disgusted look on his face, as if he wanted to see me locked away forever. A female officer was standing to the other side of me, almost looking through me and not engaging in the process at all. The fourth officer was typing on a laptop, his back to me.

The inquiry continued. Why was I there? Had I done this before? Did I drive myself? Did I have drugs on me or in my car?

After 15 minutes of questions, they told me I would be released without bail but that I had to book myself prior to my court date. That entailed a visit to the police station for a mug shot and fingerprints. They handed me a slip of paper confirming these details and walked me out into the hallway and to the stairwell. As I began to walk away, the lead officer called me back and asked me to turn around with my back to the wall. He took my picture, and then I was free to go.

It took a lifetime to walk down those two flights of stairs. When I exited the building, the light from the sun flooded my eyes and stabbed them as if it were wielding daggers. My entire body was cold, shaking, vibrating. My eyes were open wide, and I couldn't even blink despite the pain of the light. I sat in my car, again gripping my steering wheel. My mind jumped all the way back to how I started the day—dreading things that hadn't happened yet.

I shook myself back to reality. As I was driving, I had one eye on my phone to search for the phone number of a criminal defense attorney. I left a message for a lawyer and tossed my phone into the floorboard. The drive home took forever, mostly because I was driving incredibly slowly. Trying to gather myself. To put myself back together. I had a date with my family to watch the Cardinals play the Cubs in the National League playoffs. I had to hold it together. It was possibly the last normal family night we'd ever have together, and I didn't want to miss out on it. All my problems could wait until tomorrow. That had been the story of my life, so why not play it forward one more day.

CHAPTER 2

Happy Family Time

The flashlight beams cut through the night sky in search of life. They danced up and down, vibrating in loose grips as feet shuffled quickly, sweeping the area in front of them.

I peered from behind a rock wall, my heart beating. Sweat was dripping from my forehead. It was a sticky summer evening; the air was thick with humidity. The collar of my shirt was wet. I tilted my head to the side and then craned around the side of the wall, peering out toward the approaching lights.

And then I heard it, whistling through the air, a red glow tracking its course. It struck just to the left of where I was hiding.

"You missed!" I yelled as I rolled from behind the wall and charged across the park, much to the amusement of my two sons. They belly laughed as they sprinted in the opposite direction, doing their best to be small targets as I returned fire. The glow-in-the-dark bows and arrows were a hit. I pivoted and saw my wife cutting across the swing set area. I abandoned my chase of the kids and cut her off at the pass, drilling her ankle with a glowing green arrow. And then I was hit. From behind. My oldest had retreated just long enough for me to be distracted with his mom, and then he had flanked me on the backside and let fly a perfect shot. Right in the back. More belly laughter. We were the only ones at the park, but we were filling it with light and joyful sounds.

As usual, I was taking in the moment, as I did all moments like this. Happy family time. But I was also grieving in the moment, like I did most moments like this.

Happy family time. It could end in an instant. I could be exposed for the fraud I was. No peace. So many secrets. So much harm. No turning back. I couldn't undo it. I was stained. And while I appreciated the whole "white as snow" thing, just because God would cleanse me didn't mean that anyone here on earth would. For the longest time, it was more important that other people saw me without serious flaws than it was to receive God's forgiveness. As I continued to stuff emotions down deep inside, the darkness attached to me. I was one with it. Always felt it resting on my shoulder. Sticking to my skin. Seeping into my pores. I felt anything but clean.

I knew this wasn't real, these happy memories I was trying to stockpile. These experiences were fleeting and flimsy. They could be destroyed in the space between two breaths. Instead, all I had was an illusion. All I had was a moment of blissful joy colored by the truth I carried with me—that I was a fraud. A fake. A fool. None of this was real. That's what my addiction told me. It was a nice fantasy. But it wasn't real life. Even the memories I would carry forward would be lies and implications of a life that wasn't lining up.

I had been twisted so that fantasy became reality, and reality became fantasy. I didn't really know if I was coming or going. I couldn't find the truth about myself in all this. Couldn't get out of the death spiral. Couldn't get out from under the truckload of sin I had dumped on myself. Couldn't shake the voices in my head that told me I was unlovable and not enough, that everything had gone too far.

In a few short months, I'd be sitting in handcuffs in a hotel room, the voices inside saying, *We told you so.* They would be declaring the end of my fantasy world when a happy family played in the park with me. They would tell me my hope was over. That's the progression I was to follow. The last few steps in my diseased state. To feel like it was the end of the rope.

But God had other plans for me.

CHAPTER 3

It Hits the Fan

Praying for you.

That's all my friend's text message said. That's all it had to say. Less than 24 hours had passed since my arrest, and already people were hearing about what had happened. As I read the text, my heart started pounding in my throat, and for the first time in forever, I felt alive. Panicked and completely freaked out, yes. But alive. It was as if I had just exploded up from being underwater, gasping for breath, arms flailing, eyes fluttering as I searched for shore or a flotation device of some kind. I felt as if I was re-entering the world from the depths of darkness.

But I also felt as if I was going to throw up. I squeezed my phone, my eyeballs bulging. I paced my bedroom. I tapped my phone on my forehead. I raised my eyes to the ceiling, closed them, opened them, closed them. Took deep breaths. Finally, I texted my wife who was about to teach a class at her fitness studio. I told her I needed to talk to her.

She responded immediately that she was already on her way home. She already knew. Shit had hit the proverbial fan.

I thought I would have a little time to organize my thoughts and handle the situation with a clear mind and some carefully chosen words. That wasn't how it played out. The day before, when the police officer had stopped me in the hallway and snapped a quick photograph, I thought it was just for their records. As it turned out, it was for the local news. My name, photo, and address were prominently displayed on television that evening, and again in the morning newspaper. In an instant, I was exposed. My secret life, my alter ego, my darkness, my sin, all served up on a platter for the entire community. It didn't take long for my story to spread widely to most people who knew me well. Including my wife. All the hurt, betrayal, and nonsense I needed to take responsibility for, and ask forgiveness for, and I didn't even get to be the one who opened the dialogue with her. She found out about the arrest from someone else.

I'll never forget the look on her face when she arrived at the condo we were renting, which was a horrible dump. A temporary stop on our way to our dream house, which was under construction. It would be our long-term residence where happy memories and a joyful life were supposed to be waiting. She entered the front door, pale, washed out, her eyes pleading as she asked, "Is it true?"

I could only respond with two words. "I'm sick."

In that moment, I realized those two words were true, more true than any words I'd spoken to anyone in a very long time.

I used to think of sin in terms of darkness, back alleys, deserted corners. Deep down in a hole. Somewhere in the underbelly. Something you wallow in.

What I've come to realize is that sin is really more like a desolate height—our debauchery on display, high upon a hill in plain view. The juxtaposition of these two seemingly opposite words—*desolate* and *height*—is painfully poetic.

My journey, which began the day it all hit the fan, started from a desolate height, partly because of things I was chasing, and partly because of things I was running from. There I had sat, high on this hill, wondering how no one could see the real me. Wondering if maybe they could. I still didn't have the faith required to jump or descend one shaky step at a time down the side of the mountain. I was too high. Too far gone. Too damaged.

In his book *Mountains of the Mind*, Robert Macfarlane examines our longstanding fascination with, and hypnotic draw toward, mountains. For centuries, men have risked and sacrificed their lives attempting to scale the world's tallest natural monuments. I find many parallels to Macfarlane's descriptions of the mystical allure of mountains and the journey we take toward our desolate heights.

In discussing Mount Everest, Macfarlane paints a picture of slopes "studded with modern corpses." He also talks about the Death Zone, an altitude bracket where "the human body enters a gradual but unstoppable process of degeneration."[1]

Gradual, but unstoppable degeneration. Yep, that's exactly what the desolate height can feel like. The air grows thin, and your brain slows down. Your thoughts are thick and foggy. You are disoriented. Gradually falling apart from the inside. You arrive at your desolate height long before you are aware enough to feel trapped by it. Some people spend decades lost in the ether, numbed, stumbling around in the darkness, completely unaware. This is the Death Zone.

And the first step to breaking free is to realize you are enslaved. Conventional wisdom would tell you it's fairly easy to know when you have been cast into slavery, but you and I both know that you can serve a master without being fully aware of what is happening. You can be trapped inside a cage and be all too comfortable in your self-made prison.

CHAPTER 4

Birth of an Addiction

Addiction, as I see it, occurs when we are unable to appropriately engage with our emotions. We inaccurately identify the solution to our problems and form habits and compulsions that take on lives of their own over time and refuse to quit, even when we no longer see the value our habits have to offer. It's a gradual ascent, the climb toward addiction. It moves at a glacial pace. Addiction is cunning and methodical. It requests one small concession, one small contradiction at a time. It never gets greedy. It just asks for a little more, then a little more. Then one day, you peer toward the place where your life is supposed to be, and you realize you're lost.

Do You Know You're Not Alone?

If you are battling addiction or trying to help a loved one, you are not alone. You are not even the minority. Consider the following statistics:

- 47% of US adults exhibit addictive behaviors.[1]
- 68% of the population is overweight or obese.[2]
- One in six boys has been sexually abused.[3]
- One in six women has been raped.[4]
- 40 million people are addicted to alcohol, drugs, or nicotine.[5]
- In 2016 alone, approximately 60,000 people died from drug overdoses.[6]

- 30,000 people commit suicide each year.[7]
- Prostitution is an $18-billion annual industry in the United States.[8]
- 64% of men have watched pornography in the past month.[9]
- $740 billion is the annual societal cost of alcohol, tobacco, and drugs from "crime, lost work productivity, and health."[10]
- The United States has 5% of the global population and 25% of the world's prison population.[11]

What do all of these stats have in common? They all provide evidence that most, if not all, of us are struggling with significant issues that stem from unmet needs, unresolved trauma, and untapped emotions.

Where Does Addiction Come From in the First Place?

Some really smart people conducted a research study recently and determined this shocking truth: The more pain you are in, the easier it is to develop an addiction. Please insert sarcasm here. In this study, the researchers found that specifically, the risk of opioid addiction is greater among patients who are experiencing more pain.[12]

It's one of those obvious outcomes that isn't surprising at all. Of course, it makes sense that the more pain you are in, the more likely you are to over-medicate and develop an unhealthy attachment to the substance or behavior that eases or temporarily erases your discomfort. For far too many people, that pain starts at an early age. And the consequences are devastating. In a foundational study called the Adverse Childhood Experiences (ACE) Study, the Centers for Disease Control and Prevention and Kaiser Permanente[13] confirmed that two-thirds of individuals have experienced at least one ACE (adverse childhood experience), while more than one in five have had to absorb three or more. The study also found that the more ACEs you have, the more likely it is that you will experience negative outcomes in health and well-being such as alcoholism, depression, sexually transmitted diseases, and chronic conditions such as heart disease.

In his book *Chasing the Scream*, Johann Hari talks about a famous experiment called Rat Park that has significant implications for how people view addiction and what the real cause of addiction is. Here's a quick thumbnail. In previous research, rats isolated in separate cages were presented with two water bottles. One was laced with heroine, the other was pure water. The isolated rats drank from the drugged water day after day until it killed them. It happened over and over again.

They tried the same experiment in a cage where groups of rats were provided plenty of food, toys, and other rats to play with—basically a rat utopia. Interestingly, the rats in this Rat Park tried the drugged water but opted for the clean water and did not develop an addiction to the drug. Even more telling, when researchers took a rat that had been hooked on the drugged water in an isolated cage and placed it in the community setting, it stopped drinking the drugged water and started drinking clean water instead.[14] What the research shows is that it isn't a chemical hook that causes addiction. That means you can obviously be addicted to things other than substances and that what's really driving the addiction has little or nothing to do with the "high" you're experiencing as much as the "low" you're avoiding.

What Drives Someone to Unhealthy Dependence, to Obsessive and Progressively Destructive Behavior?

So what drives someone to unhealthy dependence? It's the pursuit of not feeling, or at least feeling something else. Let's go back to Macfarlane's book on mountains. He quotes a work by Edmund Burke to explain how our mind churns pleasure out of fear. Burke suggested that whatever causes terror is also a source of the sublime—"it is productive of the strongest emotion which the mind is capable of feeling."[15] In Macfarlane's context, that helps explain why people would dare climb mountains. The risk of death, the sheer terror of being wiped off the earth, brings with it a rush like no other. You can easily get addicted to that kind of rush. We all do.

For an addict, fear is usually a constant companion. It can drive you into a search for the sublime. In euphoria, you don't feel pain. All you have to do is survive, to overcome the risk, and you get filled with this incredible, freeing, all-powerful emotion that takes everything you fear, everything else you feel, and makes them go away—at least for a little while.

The problem is that they always come back. The fears. The things we didn't want to deal with. They're still there. And they hurt worse than ever. So, we run back toward the sublime, the rush, so we can numb them again. The cycle goes on and on.

But let's back way, way up for a second. I want to map out some things for you. I think it will explain a lot. As mentioned earlier, we don't just wake up addicts one day. It is a slow, arduous climb up to the desolate height. It started a long time before you took a drink, tried a drug, viewed a pornographic image, or placed a bet on a sporting event. You see, one of the most important things to understand is that it is never about "filling in the blank." Whatever your substance or activity of choice, it's never about the thing you're addicted to. Instead, the addiction is only a symptom of a bigger problem, a deeper problem. And that problem started a long time ago.

At some point, you amassed a collection of wounds that likely consist of unmet needs, unresolved trauma, and untapped emotions. It was probably in childhood. Someone did something to you. You did something to someone else. Someone abandoned you. Or you didn't get something that's critical (love, safety, provision, affection, affirmation). Whatever happened, or didn't happen, you also probably didn't know how to appropriately process the emotion that came along with it. So you carried it around.

Over time, those unmet needs, unresolved traumas, and untapped emotions created powerful, negative self-beliefs—lies you tell yourself about your own value and about how the world sees you. Sometimes, these lies are at the level of your consciousness and almost audible. Sometimes, the lies can be as subtle as subliminal messages that torture your subconscious and fight to stay undetected.

As you move through life, these wounds demand more of your attention. They weigh on you. Most people don't have a solid understanding of what's going on. They just know they feel pain. I always felt unsettled and restless, like I was missing out on life. That was just one way my wounds and negative self-beliefs manifested themselves.

Left unchecked, the lies and wounds will demand that we deal with them somehow. Triggers will form—sights, smells, tastes, thoughts, memories—all designed to poke at our open wounds and remind us of our inadequacy. If we don't dispel the lies and mend the wounds, these triggers will force the need to develop coping mechanisms.

We will find ways to ease the pain and soothe ourselves. Quickly, our ways of coping will take solid shape in the form of idols and addictions. We think that higher powers (a relationship, a job, material possessions) will heal us and that self-medication (alcohol, drugs, shopping, sex, gambling, eating, social media, and on and on) will make the pain stop for a moment. At that point, the lies have successfully isolated us from the world around us. They form chains. They cage us.

The idols always demand more from us. They use us up and leave us empty. They will always let us down and create more pain. Meanwhile, our addictive behavior is progressing. It takes more and more to feel the effects of our chosen medication. The more we use, the higher the dose has to be, and the more frequent the next dose needs to be. In his commentary on Psalm 63, Alexander MacLaren writes, "The less you can do without it the less it does for you."[16] That's so true.

The really unfortunate part about this journey is that once we are trapped within it, the cycle perpetuates itself through the shameless use of shame. It takes us right back to the lies we already believe and uses our poor choices and our character defects as proof points, validation that the lies were correct all along, that we are not worthy, lovable, or even close to okay. We feel the shame deep in our bones. It creates more pain. We need more medicine. Then we feel more shame. Then we need more medicine. We turn to our idols. Surely, they will say we're okay. But they just demand more of us. We continue to stretch and reach for the next empty promise. But our spouse never really makes us feel whole. There never seems to be enough money or success. Everything lets us down. People, places, and things trigger harmful memories and push our buttons. It's painful. We need more medicine. We have more shame. The wounds are being salted heavily.

And we're trapped. In full ascent mode, climbing up the desolate height, marching blindly toward the Death Zone. Deteriorating and self-destructing with each ill-advised step up this abominable hill. Like Paul in Romans 7:15–21, you don't understand what you're doing. The things you want to do, the path you want to take, the decisions you want to make, you don't. Instead, you find yourself doing what you hate, making decisions that harm you. But like Paul says, "It is no longer I who do it, but sin that dwells in me" (Rom. 7:17). You are on autopilot. You've set a train in motion (or had it set in motion for you), and it's lumbering down the tracks. It's really hard to stop a train once it's at top speed.

The point is this. There's a good reason you've ended up where you are. It's not all your fault, either. I like to say I offer explanations, not excuses, when I talk about my story. That's because at the end of the day, we all can make choices. I could have chosen to get help sooner, to stop the climb up the mountain. And if I found myself incapable of stopping, I could have taken that as a red flag that I really needed more help. It's far too simple, though, to only chastise my sin and judge my wrongs without trying to understand what drove me to them.

So How Do You Cure an Addiction? Can You?

Hari says, "The opposite of addiction isn't sobriety. It's connection."[17] I believe that is an entirely accurate assessment. The moment I started focusing on the wounds driving my bad choices, the moment I started engaging with other people to help me remedy my isolation, I felt the intrigue and the pull of those past addictive tendencies release their grip.

Of course, there was some withdrawal. And there are triggers that can present themselves on any given day. But it is my firm belief that whatever form addiction takes (alcohol, drugs, sex, gambling, shopping, social media, work, relationships, etc.), the overwhelming majority of its compulsivity and unrelenting urges are severely dampened when you push through and engage with what lies beneath.

Those who simply try to stop their addictive habits, to resist their urges, find little to no long-term success. Worse yet, some just substitute one addiction for another. Have you ever seen a person stop smoking but gain 50 pounds? The point is that they are not engaging the real enemy. You have to go all the way back to the beginning of the cycle for that. Your wounds. Engaging with your wounds is the key to a life free of destructive and addictive behaviors. David Kolker, the CEO of SLO Recovery Centers, captures this well in a post he wrote for Pscyh Central in which he suggested that treatment for addiction needs to focus on "problems such as abandonment, abuse, neglect, fear and lack of self-love. These are the issues that create a perfect storm for an individual to continue acting out through addictive behavior and substances."[18]

Recovering from an addiction is not easy. It can be extremely challenging. Depending on your situation, it can require professional support, inpatient rehabilitation, and/or intensive therapy. And once you've stopped, once you've been set free, how do you ensure you never walk that road again?

While I don't fully buy into the once-an-addict-always-an-addict mantra that most 12-step groups recite, I see little harm in approaching an addiction with that sort of rigor, focus, and lifelong commitment. I don't believe the 12-step model is without fault or flaws. What I do believe is that the issues being attacked and improved through step work are critical to prevent a retreat back to idols and addictions. In the end, I believe we can cure addiction. What we can't cure is our addictive nature. We are wired for survival, for passionate pursuit, for mastery, for connection with a higher power. We are built to crave wholeness. The moment we aren't in a healthy place to respond to our emotions and our experiences, our nature will offer up alternatives that aren't in our best interest. We have to learn that there is only one type of medicine that works for us. And that is moving closer to God, closer to others, and farther away from destructive cycles of shame and sin.

CHAPTER 5

Poltergeist

It was an exciting night for sure. Dad had purchased our first VCR, and we were giving it a test run. We were actually going to watch a movie, from our living room, with no commercials. It sounded whimsical and full of fantasy. A modern-day miracle. The chosen flick was *Mr. Mom* starring Michael Keaton. My parents had really gone for an unforgettable blockbuster!

We were stuffed into the living room—my parents, my grandparents, my sister, some friends, and me—full of anticipation and wonder. My dad, standing in front of the television, wrestled with the plastic case for a moment before the movie launched into the air from its shell. He snagged it mid-air, turned it around, and stared at it for a moment. Presenting it to my mom, he muttered that the store had put the wrong movie in the case. For those who have never had the pleasure of renting movies during the VCR era, it was about a 50-50 shot that you would get home with the movie you intended to rent, at least in the early days of the technology and at least where I was from. Of course, you also had to rent your movies from the gas station. Maybe that explains it.

It was worse than the cashier just not giving us *Mr. Mom*. The movie we had instead was *Poltergeist*. Not quite appropriate for the kiddos in the room. We ranged in age from five to 10 years old, and I was the oldest. After some debate, the grownups decided they were going to watch the movie. After all, everyone was staring at the VCR as if it were some great mystery. How could they not see if it really worked? My younger sister and her friend were quickly ushered to my sister's room. The adults asked us boys if we could handle it. I lied and said yes. I was fairly certain this movie was about to scare the absolute crap out of me, but I also was intrigued by this VCR thing, and I wanted to be grown up and watch a movie from my living room. I wasn't going to miss out on our first-ever VCR experience. So my friend Bill and I stayed. He was about a year younger than I was, so I can only imagine how freaked out he must have been. My heart was pounding right from the opening scene. Before that night, the scariest movie I had ever watched was *E.T.* As it turns out, *Poltergeist* was no *E.T.*

By the time the movie was over, I had literally all but crapped myself. My parents asked if I was okay about six times during the show, and I lied and lied, and then lied some more. I told them yep every single time. Big. Fat. Lie. I was terrified. You see, I had a big tree right outside my bedroom window that resembled the one in the movie—you know, the one that comes to life and reaches through the window. Also, my great-grandmother had made a stuffed toy clown for me several years earlier. It had been buried in the bottom of my closet for the longest time. I hadn't seen it in a while, but I was freaked out at the thought of that tree and that clown. However, it was bedtime, and you didn't argue with my dad. So when he said we had to go, we did.

I tried to rummage through my closet on my way to bed, but I couldn't lay eyes or hands on that stupid clown. The wind was blowing that night, and that awful tree was shifting left and right, casting shadows on the window. How was I supposed to sleep? Luckily, or so I thought at the moment, Bill was spending the night with me. At least I wouldn't be alone. We slipped beneath the covers, and the lights were turned out. After a few minutes, I whispered to him, asking him if he was as scared as I was. All I heard was snoring. But that answered my question. I was curled up in a ball, intently watching the window behind me, the closet door in front of me, and the floor beneath me for signs of evil trees or possessed clowns. For hours, my eyes were wide open, my heart racing, my body sweating beneath the covers as I trembled. Then finally, somehow, I fell asleep.

I'm not sure how long I slept. It couldn't have been long when I was nudged awake by Bill's hand. It first bumped into my lower thigh from behind me as I slept on my side. I turned onto my back and looked over. The hand slid up my thigh and stopped right on top of my private parts. He started to fidget, moving and flexing his fingers. The sensation I felt was foreign to me. I was half asleep, but my genitals were wide awake. He slipped his hand beneath my underwear and continued to fondle me. I wasn't sure what to do. It was really weird, but it felt good. And then it happened. I ejaculated.

The force and the surprise of it frightened me greatly. I wasn't sure what had happened. I thought I was injured. I sat up hurriedly in the bed, examining this strange substance and trying to verify whether I was in medical need or not. After a few moments of helpless feelings, it seemed like everything was okay. I lay back down and curled up on my side. Bill had turned back over to his side of the bed. I couldn't even be sure he was awake for any or all of it. Then again, I am still left with questions about what happened and why, all these years later.

That night, I was violated. But something more sinister occurred, something that I just recently came to understand. That night, a painful link was formed. Fear, to orgasm, to shame. It was a loop that would repeat itself in my life for years to come. And that night was the foundation.

The late night sleepover experience was not an isolated event. It happened another handful of times the following year. Sometimes Bill initiated the contact, but on a few occasions, I started it. This was extremely confusing for me, toggling between violated and violator. The last time it happened, he yelled at me in the middle of the night to "stop being a faggot!" and then went back to sleep. Somehow, I ended up being the one with the problem, even though I wasn't the one who created it. I didn't know what else to do with that shame besides accept it, carry it with me, and try to bury it deep inside. This was the wound, a valley cut into my soul that would not heal on its own. It was the beginning of a 30-year climb to a desolate height. And there was no way for a boy my age to understand any of it.

CHAPTER 6

Elephants

Elephants. What majestic, massive creatures! There are few beings on earth that represent strength, power, and brute force as well as this animal.

So, it is always surprising to see an elephant at the circus restrained only by a small chain on its leg. You would think such an animal could break the chain easily, yet there it is, safely secured and bound in place.

Based on my best Google research, the reason such a small chain can constrain such a big animal is this. When the elephant was young, a chain was placed around its leg, the other end fastened to the trunk of a tree. After several attempts to wander past the boundary imposed by the chain, the elephant realized it couldn't break free, and it adjusted accordingly. When fully grown, the same elephant is still restrained by the same chain, despite the fact that the elephant could easily rip it apart. It has been programmed to believe the chain is too strong. Resistance is futile. The chain wins.

Each of us was designed to be a powerful elephant who lives strong and has a dramatic impact on the world around us, yet most of us are led around by a small chain so the world can witness our weakness. Our chains come in the form of self-limiting beliefs and spirals of shame. They have imprisoned us for as long as we can remember.

And just like elephants, we have long memories. It's funny, I sometimes leave the living room and forget what I needed before I get to the kitchen, but I never forget for one second any significant transgression, failure, trauma, or shame-filled regret I've experienced during my time on this planet. I specifically interpreted unfortunate and traumatic experiences from my childhood as a permanent mark on my own self-worth. The incidents of sexual abuse in particular created a belief in me that I was unclean, that I was unworthy compared to others. I convinced myself that anyone who found out the truth about me would abandon me—that I was less than. That I should be ashamed of my truth. These memories created chains that tied me down. I internalized lies, actions, mistakes, and sins as definitions of who I was and as clear verdicts aimed at my self-worth, my value, and my future potential. I've met a lot of people who have done the same.

We place ourselves in bondage. We accept future limitations based on past truths. We don't for a second stop to think that we might be stronger now or that we could grow stronger. We are defined by a past we can't forget. We can't break free from the chains, despite the fact that we could shed them fairly easily.

It is a very effective tactic that Satan uses against us. He takes a "truth" about us not being worthy and then uses that deeply seeded belief in unnatural ways. He constructs a chain that says because of our faults, we can't successfully overcome sin. Because of our faults, we have failed and will fail again. Because of our faults, we aren't worthy to be loved by others or used by God. I don't think many of us consciously think like this, but it's the internal hopeless feeling that many of us have about our current situations. We haven't fully trusted God, and we've failed on our own, so we just pace in circles around a tree, accepting the limitations imposed on us by ourselves and by our surroundings.

Forgetting the Past

No, dear brothers, I am still not all I should be, but I am bringing all my energies to bear on this one thing: Forgetting the past and looking forward to what lies ahead, I strain to reach the end of the race and receive the prize for which God is calling us up to heaven because of what Christ Jesus did for us" (Phil. 3:13–14 TLB).

Ever tried forgetting the past? It's okay if you can't. In fact, I would encourage you not to do so. It's not that you must forget the past as much as reinterpret it. After all, the chains are real—the power of the chains is the illusion you need to overcome. God does not hold on to the sins of the past, yours or other people's. You shouldn't either. Release them, and you release their hold on you. It's not that you are forgetting. You can even still use those memories in positive ways. But what you are doing is drawing a line in the sand and declaring that they won't define you, won't control you, won't chain you any longer.

"Some things go. Pass on. Some things just stay....You know. Some things you forget. Other things you never do."[1] In this quote from Toni Morrison's book *Beloved*, the main character, Sethe, wrestles with how she can prevail over the trauma of slavery while the memories are still alive and well. How do we overcome the past when it still holds an influence over us?

You don't need to erase the past, block it out, or forget it. You need to embrace it, use it, and let it appropriately inform your future. Who we are is a direct result of where we've been and what we've experienced. Good. Bad. Ugly. Every mistake, every poor choice, every act of abuse or betrayal or trespass. God will use it all to design us and equip us for His purpose. He will work within the wreckage of every person, reassembling broken pieces, forging strength from weakness, finding perfection in the imperfect.

That means many of us need to closely examine how we treat the past, because we've likely made the mistake of letting memories (particularly bad ones) continue to derail us. To hold us down. To oppress us. To define us. To strip hope, peace, and joy from us. To poison our thoughts. To haunt our dreams.

We have to stop using our memory as a torture device or a shaming technique, as evidence to substantiate the lies we tell ourselves, as an escape from reality, as an excuse for a pity party, as a cage that renders us helpless and depressed, as a way to keep score and justify our victimhood, or as a glass ceiling that limits our future potential.

Instead, we should leverage our memory positively to retain and recall the lessons we've learned, to keep us humble before God, to keep us filled with gratitude as a means of instruction for others and ourselves, as a counterbalance to irrational present thoughts or future tripping, as a detailed ledger of our strengths and our weaknesses, as a way to measure how far we've come and how far we still need to go.

Memories can be an extraordinarily powerful tool for our healing and for our health. They can also be a cancer that gnaws us from the inside and blinds us from all that is beautiful about ourselves, our lives, and the world around us. Some memories leave us quickly and don't hang around. But some stay. I strongly believe any memories strong enough to stay with us (good or bad or ugly) are to be used for a greater purpose. They have magical powers waiting to be harnessed. But like any superhero, we have to use that power for good and not in destructive ways.

I'll use a rather benign and innocuous example to illustrate this point. My older son and I share a similar memory. His will not torment him. Mine did. When I was about nine years old, I was playing in a post-season baseball tournament. We were the top seed. We had gone through the entire season undefeated and were in the championship game. I had enjoyed an all-star season as a pitcher and a first baseman. I was one of the main reasons we were undefeated. Here it was, in the last inning, two outs, men on base, and all I had to do was get a hit for us to win it all. I struck out.

For those who aren't sports enthusiasts, one of the worst feelings in the world is striking out in baseball. The only thing worse is ending a game with a strikeout. The only thing worse than that is ending a championship game with a strikeout. And the only thing worse than that is ending a championship game with a strikeout while not swinging your bat. In that moment, a memory was deeply embedded in me. That feeling of inadequacy and failure would haunt me for most of my sports career. I carried it like luggage on an airplane. I put immense pressure on myself to perform at an extremely high level athletically. I had to be perfect. And if my team didn't win and I wasn't perfect, I beat myself up over it.

My older son was in a similar situation recently. He was playing on a Little League team. He had managed to play 20 games during the regular season without striking out once. Throughout the season, he was the most consistent contributor to his team. A leader. The guy everyone could count on to deliver the goods. And there he was. In the playoffs. Late in the game with the bases loaded. Down one run. Two outs. With three balls and two strikes. He swung. And he missed. At least he went down swinging, right?

The difference between these two memories is that I was in a position to help him put his "failure" into perspective. He was able to use it as a learning experience. He was able to appreciate the fact that he went 20 games without a strikeout. He will use that memory for good, not to his own detriment. He won't process it as trauma. Not the way I did.

It's all about perspective. Regardless of how much trauma lives on in your memory, today you are blessed beyond measure. Air filling your lungs. Beauty filling your eyes. Music filling your ears.

You can choose joy. You can leave the pain behind while you carry its scars. You can use the past to create more of the joy you seek now. Trust me, it's not easy. It's a daily discipline. I need constant reminders that it's the meaning I've attached to the memories that is the real problem.

Let's revisit our elephants for a moment. Have you seen what happens when a captive elephant realizes it can break free? Or when one of these massive beasts finally gets enough of being dragged around by such a small chain?

A therapist of mine once showed me a series of videos of elephants freaking out and breaking free—going on rampages, throwing people, cars, and whatever else was in their path out of their way. The power of an elephant that breaks its chains is something worthy of shock and awe. The sheer strength of this animal!

That's the power we have inside. That's what freedom feels like. God wants us to take these weak chains that have bound us for so long and rip them to pieces. He wants us to flex our muscles and push through obstacles. He wants us to rush to freedom.

Your past. Your addictions. Your emotions. Your idols. Your obsessions. Whatever you obey and serve, that will enslave you (Rom. 6:16).

These chains are real. Their power, however, is largely imagined.

CHAPTER 7

Sentencing

On my phone, it read, "Mom cell" with the message, "Please call."

I was standing in line to be booked, so for once I had a legitimate excuse not to call her back. As I waited for the officers, I watched a guy on a pay phone yelling about getting out on bond and complaining about his "stupid wife." I caught myself thinking, *I'm not like that. I don't belong here.* An inmate shuffled through in his stripes, picking up boxes and garbage. A wave came over me again, a self-righteous wave, and I thought, *I really don't belong here. I'm better than this.*

The irony of my situation is that in my quest to be accepted, loved for who I am, I've constantly tried to convince myself that I'm not as shitty as I think I am. At the same time, I'm full of vanity, even in the face of feeling unworthy at my core. Within me, there's always been a constant battle between delusions of grandeur and low self-esteem. In order to deal with the feelings of unworthiness, I try to project what would make me worthy and obsess on making that happen. If I could just do or be this or that, if I could just make it to a certain rank or place, if I could just...

The black residue temporarily stained the tips of my fingers. I had been fully booked and was free to leave. As I exited each of the doors, hearing the buzz and the clang of them locking behind me, I shivered. Stepping out into the bright sun, I looked above to the clouds with wanting eyes, searching for something. Anything. Worrying that I might possibly have to go back to the place I just left. That maybe I'd be the one shuffling through the halls picking up trash. I pressed forward, climbed into my truck, and tucked my police paperwork into my glove compartment. I glanced at my phone. Mom cell. Please call. Nope, not today.

A few weeks later I stood before a judge in a criminal court. Flanked by men and women in orange jumpsuits, paired off in hand-cuffs. Behind me was a courtroom full of DUIs and drug offenses and other untold crimes, some of which required bail in the six-figure range. I stood behind the podium on weak, wobbly knees, shaking on the inside and sweating on the outside. I looked the woman judge in the eyes as she explained my sentencing for soliciting a prostitute. I was getting off easy, in legal terms. Six months of probation with only a few conditions, and then I could have my file expunged so the offense was no longer part of my personal record. But as I stood in that courtroom, listened to my sentencing, and looked into this woman's eyes as I admitted guilt for a crime against all women, I was not getting off easy at all. I felt deep shame, remorse, and guilt. I also felt overwhelming clarity. I was here—in a courtroom—being sentenced for a crime. Me. This was really happening. I had to repeat this sequence in my mind several times to make absolutely sure I fully understood that this wasn't fantasy. It was reality—cold, hard, reality.

I lost a great deal of pride that day, but I found freedom. And I found my fight. From that moment, I clearly understood my desolate height. More importantly, I caught a glimpse of my potential, and my purpose.

CHAPTER 8

Runaway

The bicycle was fighting me for control as I peddled hard up a tall hill on a country backroad. Hanging off each handlebar was a duffle bag stuffed with essentials, at least those items that would seem necessary for an 11-year-old. I churned along, my legs aching, my arms flexing as I wrestled with the wobbly front wheel, barely maintaining balance. My destination was only a few miles away, but these heavy bags draped over my Huffy were proving to be a challenge. I continued to press ahead, my orange-and-rust-colored cycle trudging along. A faded and worn Dallas Cowboys decal hugged the center bar, displaying my childhood football loyalties. The seat was slightly torn, and the back was riddled with teeth marks from the family dog. This ride had seen its fair share of action. It needed some work, but it would get me where I was going.

I pulled up to the sloped driveway of my best friend's house, slid off the side of my bike, and then pushed it up the hill. As I circled around back to the garage, his mom came out to greet me. I informed her that I had run away from home. She once had told me that if I ever needed to run away, I could come live with them. So here I was, taking her up on her offer. To be honest, I don't recall how the offer was on the table to begin with since it wasn't like I had any legitimate reason to flee from home. In any event, the offer had been extended and now accepted.

She smiled and said she was glad I trusted her. But after telling me to come inside with my bags, she grabbed the home phone. I could only hear her side of the conversation, but that was enough. She said, "Hey, yes, he is here. Yes. Looks like it. Can he stay and play for an hour? Ok, I will. Sure. Bye."

Five minutes later, I was headed home, ratted out by my best friend's mom. I didn't even get to stay and play an hour. I thought she meant it, that I could stay with them. She did not. I guess maybe she had made an agreement with my mom. I don't know.

I don't remember exactly why I ran away that day. Not specifically. But I know what I was running away from, and it wasn't my parents. The preceding year had not been kind to me. And no one knew anything about it. The shame stirred inside me as I held tightly to the secrets. They were weighing on me, like duffle bags on handlebars.

I also don't remember what my parents said to me when I got back home. I remember sitting on the picnic table in the backyard. I remember being in trouble. I remember it being my sister's birthday, maybe? The memory isn't clear. I only remember that I peddled my heart out that morning to get away from something. And I remember that feeling of intense betrayal when I was immediately returned home.

It was the first time I remember wanting to run and hide, wanting to change scenery to make it all better. For years, I would feel unsettled. I would move. And move again. And then want to move again. Run away. Always believing that changing my location, my job, my situation would heal the pain I carried inside.

So for a long time, I wandered through my life as that 11-year-old boy, the same one whose idea of freedom was to stuff two duffle bags, hook them to a bicycle, and peddle five miles down the road to his best friend's house. He believed no one would ever find him there, that he could hide from all his problems, that he had solved everything.

That 11-year-old mind was where my emotional faculties froze, failing to mature. That was the year my development was stunted in a sense. It was where my abandonment issues started to thrive, where shame started to define my soul, when the restless feelings, and the delusions of grandeur, and the feelings of inadequacy, and the need to perform, and the fear of not being enough would all start pressing in on me, from the inside and from the outside. I was being shaped into a codependent, shame-filled addict. At the ripe old age of 11, I learned some really bad coping mechanisms. I could have no understanding of the shadow it all would cast on my future.

CHAPTER 9

The Flood

It felt like water was rising just beneath my nostrils, like I was enclosed in a tiny chamber relentlessly filling with liquid. As the air escaped, as the water climbed, I felt like I was going to die. I felt as if my heart were going to stop. I held my face poker straight, but inside was only fear. I wanted to run, and run fast. I wanted to be anywhere other than there. I wanted out of the trap. I was panicked, claustrophobic, and entirely uncomfortable. But there was no way out.

We stood face to face. Eyeball to eyeball. Less than two feet apart from one another. Just me and a complete stranger. Nice enough guy, I was guessing. About my height. About my age. Groomed beard. Looked the part of a creative artist of some sort. Seemed quiet. A little shifty. Probably just as uncomfortable as I was. I shot a glance to my left and my right, trying to observe the other pairings in the room. Hoping to see others who were as obviously uncomfortable as I was. Then I retrained my eyes on the man fidgeting in front of me. The question hung heavily in the air. Neither of us appeared strong enough to pick it up and address it.

Our assignment in this particular exercise was to look at the man who stood across from each of us and tell him the one thing we were most afraid for him to know. We were in a standoff, each hoping the other would go first. Finally, he broke the silence.

"The thing I wouldn't want you to know is…." He took a long pause, swallowed hard, mustered up his courage again, and finished his sentence. "…is that I struggle with being attracted to other men."

It was obvious that his attraction to other men was something he didn't want to be true. It was the cause of deep shame. It was something he fully expected to be judged harshly for. I received his confession and stood in silence for a moment, quietly nodding my head to affirm I heard him. His eyes searched mine, swimming in small circles, pupils dilating, his cheeks filling with color as he awaited my reaction and my return confession.

Inside I squirmed, contorted, twisted myself in knots. So many things I could say in response, so many things I could confess. So many options.

"Sometimes, I feel invisible," I blurted. "I sometimes feel like no one can really see me, that I don't matter. That's the thing I'd least like you to know."

It was a cop out for sure. In the moment, I lacked the bravery to confess my darkest secrets to a complete stranger, despite the fact that he had entrusted his pain with me. Despite the fact that I could relate to the nature of his struggle. Instead, I took the easy road and in so many words told him, "Thanks for sharing, now I'm gonna pass. It was fun talking though."

As soon as I released the words from my lips, I watched him shrivel and slump. I saw the energy leave his body. I saw hope turn to shame. I saw his eyes panic and scream. The color retreated from his cheeks, and his entire face grew pale. His throat expanded and contracted as he swallowed hard again. He had gone out on a limb, taken a chance. He had been transparent and vulnerable. And I had not. We were the first pair to complete the exercise. All other pairings seemed to be engaging in dialogue. We just stood there awkwardly—me covering all my secrets, and him feeling naked and exposed for sharing his. I've never had someone look at me with that level of disappointment in their eyes. Not even my wife when I first confessed all the harm I'd caused in my addiction.

I still wake up some nights, jarred by his face in my dreams. In processing this experience with a therapist, I was told to release my shame and guilt over this incident, that it wasn't my responsibility if he was hurt by my inability to be vulnerable. I wasn't in a place where I was healthy enough to do that. He had stepped out in faith. He was working through his issues. Sure, I could have made it easier for him, but I didn't. And that's okay.

I hold tightly to that memory, though I do have some guilt. I do worry that I was an obstacle to his healing. But mostly I remind myself that over the years, I've walked by hundreds of men who are in the same position. Searching for someone safe. Desperate for confirmation that they aren't alone in their struggles. Searching for answers or at least someone who will have an authentic conversation with them about what's going on inside. I've missed countless opportunities to share my story, my heart, and any small nuggets of wisdom I've been able to squirrel away over time.

I remember him because I need to model his courage. I need to go first. I need to share my secrets, continue to shed light on them in order for others to see that there is hope and healing when they drag what's in the dark into the light. I remember him, that look on his face, because I've felt that way. I've seen others feel that way. We all have felt that way. Naked. Exposed. Raw. Aching. In agony. Feeling judged, rejected, and unaccepted.

My encounter with this guy was the kickoff to an intense two days with a group of men where the mission was to break you down and build you back up. It was a strategically designed experience to strip away all the walls guys typically put up in order to engage at a deeper level and expose some of our most basic wounds. It was intentionally kept a secret for the most part in terms of what it was really about. You had to be invited by someone, and then you were told as little as possible to get you committed. It was a secret society kind of thing. The person who invited you would just tell you they felt it was something you should do. A friend of mine recruited me, and despite red flags flying all around, I said okay. I knew full well it would be out of my comfort zone, but something inside made me say yes anyway.

We were at an old, rundown campsite with a few decrepit sleeping cabins, complete with rusted springs stabbing out the sides of the mattresses and the fragrant aroma of mold, mud, and mildew thick in the air. On the ground in a tent would have been more comfortable.

A rather harmless looking river hugged the side of the campsite. The site itself was set a mile back from the nearest road in a shallow bowl of land. It had been raining since we arrived the night before. The river was starting to spill over into the grounds. It was a sloshy walk back and forth from the main meeting area to the sleeping quarters. After a while, the group combined weather reports with visual accounts and determined we were in potential danger. The water kept rising. It was lapping at the bases of the cabins, climbing by the minute. The rain wasn't easing. If anything, it was gaining strength. After a healthy debate among manly men, the group decided to abandon the site and head for higher ground. We almost stayed. And we almost drowned.

As the last truck fishtailed its way out of the campground, the river lost its edge. A very short time later, the campground was gutted by a torrent of violent water. Our sleeping cabin was lifted from its foundation and washed downstream. Large trees punctured the meeting space. A trailer home was dropped into the middle of camp from parts unknown. Later, they even found a goat launched multiple feet into a tree. I'm not exaggerating. A goat. In a tree.

As a group, we gathered in the music room of a nearby elementary school, safe but still not completely appreciating the danger we had just escaped. The weekend would go on.

I had been stressed all weekend, sick to my stomach. I was so far out of my comfort zone I was physically twitching. And now, I was soaked to the bone on top of it. The late afternoon brought about what I can only describe as an intense, role playing, cathartic therapy session that was just short of an exorcism. It was serious business. The exercise involved me stripping down naked (symbolically ridding myself of negative messages) and crawling through a tunnel of men to be "reborn." On the other side, if I made it that far, I was to clothe myself with new, positive messages. Out of context, this all sounds crazy, I'm sure. You've heard the saying, "You had to be there." Well, you had to be there.

I need validation, affirmation, and approval. I've been screaming for it my entire life. I've struggled mightily with it. And I had let it consume me. Before this weekend, I hadn't fully articulated that to myself, the actual wound I was dealing with, much less understood where it came from and how it had shaped me. What I learned on this weekend while a torrential downpour pushed our group all over Nashville was just how deep and dark and infected my wound had become. As I stood there in a room full of dudes with only my undies on (no, I did not make it all the way to commando status), I realized this gaping hole in me had been the most significant culprit in my struggles. I felt less than. And that feeling of inadequacy had spurred bad behaviors and poor judgment. It had propelled my overly competitive nature. It had filled my head with audacious dreams of success and accomplishment so I could finally measure up.

In this moment, despite being enlightened, I was still not rescued from my bondage. The visions would start. Visions from God. Highly specific visions. But the slavery of sin and addiction would get much worse before things got better. There were still pieces of the puzzle I had yet to put into place. I didn't fully understand what was happening in me, what the addiction was really all about. I didn't have a label for it. I just knew I'd done things I was ashamed of, things I had no explanation for, and the list was growing.

The flood occurred four years before my moment of truth, the day of the arrest. It was a time when I was beginning to really struggle with my sex addiction. I had already committed enough sins and inflicted enough pain and betrayal in my marriage to feel like I was the worst kind of bad person. I was the kind of bad person whose life everyone else thought was in order.

I prayed nightly as I soaked in the bathtub for God to take this burden from me. To heal me from my past and my transgressions. To mend my wounds. To use my pain in beautifully positive ways. I prayed for Him to order my steps, to speak clearly into me and to definitively show me the path and plan He had for my life. Each time, without fail, He responded with a crystal clear picture of me helping others who had wrestled with addiction, abuse, and abandonment. And every time, I waved Him off. You see, for that picture to come through, I'd have to sacrifice some things I wasn't prepared to let go of—specifically, my family. For me to help others in any meaningful way, my wife would have to know about my struggles and my past transgressions. There was no way she'd stay after discovering what a self-absorbed asshole I'd been, what a steaming pile of a man I was, what a wretched, broken, dirty sinner I was. What a disgrace. What a fake. What a hypocrite. No, I couldn't accept losing her, so I told God, *Thanks, but no thanks.*

Several years later, as I sat in the center of a so-called hurricane that I more or less had spun up all by myself, a good friend delivered a message directly from God. I told him this story, of how I sat in that tub nightly, and all God would do for me was serve up that one vision of a future where I was helping others fight similar fights. And I said the same thing to him, specifically how I couldn't lose my family to gain what God had prepared as my path forward. He asked me this question: "Did God ever say that you had to lose your family?"

I sat in silence, staring at him but through him. This was not my friend's question. It was God's. The answer, of course, was no, because at no time did God ever suggest I'd have to forfeit my family to serve Him in this way. I made that part up myself. I jumped to that conclusion. I bought into that lie, likely with help from Satan. And that one artificial obstacle kept me caged for another half a decade.

We all know the story of Abraham being asked by God to sacrifice the life of his son Isaac whom he had placed above God in his heart. We all know the end of the story. Abraham is obedient and is about to carry out the act when God presses pause and says he doesn't have to go through with it.

That's where I was. My wife and my two sons were the primary obstacles to my getting better and following God. I had placed the importance of maintaining and protecting those relationships above God. My family had become an idol, a powerful idol. And I was trying to save it myself because God's plan sounded, quite frankly, like it was ill-conceived with no chance of success. Bringing my sin into the light and sharing my story would result in an immediate destruction of my marriage. It would be over in an instant. If that's what God had in mind, I was not interested.

My plan, as it turns out, wasn't very well-constructed either. My approach was to push my sin further into the dark, lock it away, and try to hold it back without telling anyone or getting help. I would just pray that it would all disappear in the morning like a bad dream and that God would let me start fresh. Meanwhile, my personal demons raged on, and I didn't even fully understand the battle I was fighting. I was an addict who didn't realize he was addicted. I saw no hope. No way out. No path down from the desolate height.

Meanwhile, my wife, whom I had placed above God, was planning to divorce me. The idol in my life, the person I was worshipping and placing on the highest pedestal, didn't even want to be in a relationship with me. How could that be? Surely I was showering her with affection and attention and making her feel all-powerful, right? After all, she was the one thing too precious, too valuable for me to place at risk because of what God was asking of me. Nope. Not even close. As it turns out, as I grew darker, I was pushing her farther away.

With every transgression, hurtful word, burst of anger, bout of depression, or slothful response to pulling my weight around the house or in the relationship, I drove a wedge between us. I just kept forcing it deeper and wider. And in my sickness, in my stupidity, I would stand on the far side and shout to her, "Why am I not worthy of your desire? Why don't you want me? Why can't you show me?" This is the world I was living in, creating my own issues as a response to my wounds. I was spinning up a self-fulfilling prophecy. I was self-destructing, ensuring that the things I wanted most would remain out of reach. But they still would be more alluring, more important, and a higher priority than God and His calling.

And the saddest part about it? I had no idea what was really happening. I had no idea how far I'd gone. I had no idea my marriage was on the verge of ending.

It turns out that God was allowing me to make this sacrifice on my own terms, if and until He deemed it necessary to take matters into His own hands.

CHAPTER 10

Sidekick

When I was a kid, getting your hands on pornography was a lot like hunting for eggs on Easter. It was around and not all that difficult to find, but you did at least have to go looking. It wasn't the constant barrage and predatory practices typical of today's environment where images come looking for you. Still, there was pornography. Some of it was handed down to my friends from older brothers. Some of it was stashed in a grownup's drawer or garage. Some was available to purchase or rent from storeowners who didn't seem to care how old you were, as long as you had money.

I was exposed to porn at a young age. I think most boys are, unfortunately. And I think that's truer now than it was for the kids of my generation. Maybe, maybe not. But I remember being more confused than infatuated with the images I saw. I already had a very warped view of what sex was and how it worked. I blame a lot of that on my best friend's older brother who thought it was funny to feed us with misinformation about girls and sex and watch our young brains soak it up and get twisted in the process.

And I was very much twisted. The late-night explorations with my other friend had ended, but I was left with curiosity and confusion. On a couple of occasions, still as a kid, that curiosity got the best of me, and I succumbed to the urge of reenacting my first encounters while on sleepovers with other kids. In the middle of the night, I'd strategically reposition myself where we slept and try to find a way to have them touch me without waking them up. I recall these being very futile attempts that didn't really get anywhere. But I inherited incredible shame just from having the thoughts and trying to act on them.

There were other skeletons to place in my childhood closet. I've chosen to omit them here, not in an attempt to hide or conceal them. They just don't need to be processed publicly at the moment. But they contributed to my shame in significant ways.

Eventually, I was able to bury those urges and experiences, but their graves were shallow, and like every hokey horror movie, they would eventually come back to life, punch fists through the dirt, and demand to be reckoned with one more time.

During my childhood, my best friend significantly contributed to the low self-esteem sparked by my sexual experiences. I was his sidekick, the Robin to his Batman. And I always felt inferior to him. His family had more money. He had a pool. He was more popular. My habitual need to compare myself with people I can't compete with started right there. I recall that his words and actions continually made me feel inadequate, but honestly, who knows how much of that was real versus imagined.

It seems laughable to me now, but one example I clearly remember when I was made to feel less than happened when I wasn't allowed to have one of my friend's special Pop-Tarts®. They were chocolate with white crème filling and white icing, topped with flecks of chocolate. I don't remember what they were called, but I still can picture the box. I literally was forbidden from having any of them when I slept over at his house. They were off limits. This silly example summed up the structure of our relationship. I was a lower-class citizen, not worthy of the finer things—like vanilla-frosted, chocolate Pop-Tarts®.

Over the years, I built up resentment toward him and how I felt when I was around him. Our social circles in junior high began to separate us. I felt even more like a tagalong. Eventually, the strain was so great that we just stopped being best friends. There was never a specific fight or discussion about it. We just drifted. We went from being inseparable to both having new best friends. But that didn't stop me from comparing myself to him. If anything, it intensified the competition.

As I entered my teen years, everything seemed just fine with me. I was a straight A student, a starting outfielder for the baseball team, and first-chair trumpet in the marching band. I was dating a cheerleader. I had also tapped into my passion for writing and was receiving affirmation from classmates and teachers that it was a talent I should pursue. But inside, there was a pile of explosives waiting to be detonated, an unsteady state that just needed one solid push to set in motion a cataclysmic chain of events. My childhood had prepped me for a dumpster fire. I just needed someone to throw in a match and watch me burn.

CHAPTER 11

Therapy Session

Daybreak. A black sedan sat in an empty parking lot just ahead. Its left back bumper was bent and twisted upward like a crooked smile. The trunk was popped open. A clear blue sky lay overhead, with long thick clouds moving slowly across it. Office buildings flanked me on three sides, all uninhabited at the moment. The black sedan was the only other vehicle in sight. I noticed it didn't have a license plate. I wondered if there was something, or someone, in the trunk. I distracted myself from the appointment I was headed to and examined this mysterious car, every single detail of it. I tried to build a story around it—where it came from, why it was left here, what had happened.

Eventually, I had to turn my car off and go inside. I had been 30 minutes early when I pulled in, but my inspection of the black sedan had drained the clock, and I hadn't even realized it. I walked inside and waited. After a few minutes, a friendly face popped his head around the stairs and waved me up. I was about to unleash painful childhood memories on this complete stranger, allowing him to see the wars that raged behind my face and beneath the surface. At least that was the plan. I doubted I could go through with it. But I did.

I had returned home from the men's retreat weekend (a.k.a. the flood) ready to change my life, to face my demons head on. I stepped out in faith and shared my story with my wife the day after returning home from the retreat. Well, I shared my childhood story with her, not how it had impacted me as an adult. She was gracious and kind and loving in her response to me, but I believe it stirred up a thousand questions she avoided asking. I also told her I wanted to renew our vows and start our relationship fresh. I meant it. I wasn't capable of it at that moment, but I meant it. Somehow, I thought I could just tuck the past away in a drawer and not have to deal with it. I wanted to just look ahead and proceed with a better version of my life and leave the past all behind.

My wife and I agreed I should process the childhood trauma with a professional counselor, so here I was in his office.

I had barely entered the front door of his office before blurting out all the painful memories that scarred my childhood, the things I was most shameful of, the things that haunted me. The things that had burrowed into my subconscious and only recently had peeked their ugly heads out from beneath the gray matter. I took the confessional all the way up to young adulthood, and then I bailed on the truth, exactly as I had done with my wife a few nights before. He responded the exact same way as my wife had responded. Kind eyes, solemn, sitting quietly but leaning forward, silent, almost frozen.

"Is there anything else you'd like to share?" he asked when I had finished. There was more, but I wasn't ready. It had taken a tremendous amount of courage for me to share what I had shared already, and for some reason, it was even more damning to talk about how these experiences had shaped choices in my adult life. Looking back, I can only imagine him rolling his eyes when I wasn't looking. It had to have been so obvious that the past wasn't just in the past, or I wouldn't be sitting in his office. He knew full well there had been consequences, that these experiences had spilled over into my adult version of myself. He didn't push, though. He just let me stop the train.

After a brief pause, he collected his thoughts and spoke firmly but gently to me. He assured me that nothing I had said or done made him think badly of me. He assured me that I didn't have to be defined by these experiences. He told me there were many others who had walked a similar road.

He said all the right things that day. He gave me a couple of Bible verses that I still meditate on regularly. But he didn't help me. It's not that he was incapable of helping me. It's that he chose not to. At least that's how it felt to me. After a few sessions, he suggested I see another therapist, one who was trained in a special technique for overcoming childhood trauma. Of course, what I concluded from the referral is that once he had heard part of my story, he no longer wanted to engage with me, so he was passing the hot potato, the hot mess that was me. I took it personally.

And even though I'm convinced the next referral was not a good fit for me anyway, the poor guy never had a chance. I entered his office unwilling to receive his assistance. I sat fidgeting on his couch, with him in the chair next to me. A lamp on a small table separated us. He coiled himself up in snake-like fashion and asked me to tell him my story. So I replayed all the things I had shared with the previous therapist. And I watched as therapist #2 nodded and winced and tried a little too hard to convey his empathy and understanding.

A few appointments later, he took me through an immersive therapeutic technique that promised to separate and disrupt harmful memories and somehow reassign the emotions they carried. I was skeptical about this form of therapy, but evidently it has helped many people.

I watched as he moved his finger back and forth in front of my face. Slowly. I responded to his questions.

"Where are you?" he asked.

"I'm on the edge of a bed."

"Are you alone?"

"No, he's there too."

"What's happening?"

"We're watching TV. General Hospital. Really, it's just on."

"What else is happening?"

"He's telling me to lie down. That we are going to play a game. Just like the show. He needs to operate. I'm the patient."

"What is he doing?"

"He's pulling my pants down. And putting his mouth on me. He's getting the poison out."

"What are you feeling? Are you scared?"

"No. I think I'm confused a little. Feel weird about it. But not scared."

"What do you see around you? What color are the walls? The carpet? Are there pictures on the wall? What do you hear? Smell?"

I filled in the blanks the best I could. His finger stopped moving.

"Ok, let's do it again," he said. And so, we did. Running back through that same memory over and over and over.

I left his office with a headache, and an even more elaborate and clear memory of what happened to me at an extremely young age. I was more in touch with the beginnings of my story, but otherwise, it was not very helpful.

I endured a handful of sessions before breaking it off and retreating to the darkness again. I had made an attempt to step into the light. But I had been unsuccessful, and I felt all alone. Things would get worse, so much worse, before they would get better. Between this unsuccessful attempt to heal and my eventual arrest, I would scale my desolate height and largely waste another four years of my life in the process.

CHAPTER 12

Fire Starter

Eat. Just eat. Don't think yet. Scarf it down. Clean the plate before your mind activates, before it triggers your stomach to twist into knots, before the nausea kicks in, before you start to shiver. Food is important. Necessary even. Move the fork a little faster. Fork to mouth. Fork to mouth. Chew. Swallow. Don't linger long enough to taste it. That gives the brain an opportunity to fire up. It probably doesn't taste great anyway. Not tasty enough to risk a thought creeping in. One thought leads to two, and that leads to pain—unbearable, gut-wrenching, searing, seismic-level pain.

It was over, and I couldn't deal.

She was my first love. And the beginning of the end. We met my freshman year of college. I quickly lost my virginity to her. We dated for three years, and although we were never formally engaged, the unspoken plan was as follows: finish school, get married, have kids—live happily ever after. Something happened on the road to happily ever after, though. The insecurity and inadequacy inside of me started bubbling up. The more I cared about her, the more tightly I felt I needed to hold on to her. What I can see clearly now is that I became progressively more needy, clingy, jealous, possessive, and demanding. The more I smothered her, the more distance she needed. It began by her withholding physical intimacy. The more distance she needed, the more fear I had about losing her. Eventually, my fears were realized. The one person who had promised to always be there, who said she couldn't see a life for herself that didn't include me, the person I shared myself with in every possible way—she wanted out.

I remember the sting of her reflexive recoil in bed as I tried to touch her, that subtle shift toward the opposite corner that occurred as my hand crossed over her. I remember chasing her car after a heated argument that ended with her slamming the door and driving away. I remember finding doodles in her notebook where she had been sketching hearts and some other guy's name during classes. I remember how our mutual friends rallied around her after the breakup and how it really felt like I was the one who called it quits. Like everyone was judging me. I remember feeling violated, no different from when I was five years old and coerced into a game of hospital. And for a while, even eating was hard.

This is the exact moment in time when my ascent to my desolate height began. The anguish and hurt, the feelings of unworthiness, the fears of abandonment, were all unlocked and unleashed. They invaded my heart, soul, and mind. They dug in deep. They burrowed and hid, expressing themselves in subtle ways at first, slowly and surely taking over more of me until they were in full control of my life.

For the first few weeks after the breakup, I couldn't breathe, I couldn't think, I could barely eat. It was about this time that I discovered 900 numbers, which became a new hobby for me to break the monotony of the pain I was feeling. Before I knew it, I racked up nearly a thousand dollars on a credit card and had to creatively pay it off to avoid having to ask my parents for help with the bill. I also stumbled into another relationship with a close friend. It was great at first, almost as great as my first love. But after two years, it ended on a spring break trip to North Carolina. Six of us, all the best of buds, went skiing on a beginner's slope. On the first day, my girlfriend and I attempted to mount the ski lift to the top of the hill. My feet tangled in hers and as the carriage attempted to scoop us up, we flipped off the front of it, tumbled to the ground (about a six-foot drop) and face-planted in the snow. I'm not exaggerating when I say that everyone within a mile of that mountain stopped and stared. The operator halted the lift. Emergency personnel flocked to us. It's very fortunate that social media wasn't a thing yet, because we would have been a headliner on epic fail videos for eternity.

After shrugging off the first responders, my girlfriend marched as briskly as one can through snow, huffing and puffing the whole way. When I caught up with her on a park bench, she ended the relationship. Public humiliation from a ski lift incident was evidently the last nail in our relational coffin.

I spent the next five days sharing a backseat and a hotel room with her and our closest friends. The trip went on, even though our relationship didn't. I had nowhere to hide. So I was forced to mourn publicly. I can only imagine how pitiful I looked.

The saddest part about this story wasn't that I got dumped (by a girl) after being dumped (by a ski lift). It was that the breakup with that first girl—my first love—and the wreckage it left in its wake had set me up for a vicious cycle that played out almost half a dozen times before I finally broke it. Find a girl. Date. Get serious. Smother her. Cling. Push her away. Get desperate. Push her further. Watch her leave. Struggle to eat. And then find another girl.

From my late teens to my mid-20s, that was the cycle. The sad part is that I had no idea what role I played in the failure of these relationships. Instead, I concluded that all women were evil and that I was a serial victim of these horrible beings, lured in by promises of love only to be tortured, gutted, and left for dead. Looking back, it is beyond obvious that I was using each of these relationships to cope, to medicate, to validate. None of these women were capable of saving me, of making me feel okay, and yet that's exactly what I asked each of them to do.

And then I met the woman I would marry as I carried all these wounds, all these insecurities, all these unmet needs. It felt different for a while. But eventually, I started to develop the same anxiety, the same ominous feelings. She couldn't save me. She would abandon me. I repeated many of my past patterns. This time, she didn't leave. But she did retreat. As it turns out, that was even more painful. And it was all I needed to turn to new methods of medication.

CHAPTER 13

Starting My Own Thing

I opened my eyes to a sideways view of the sidewalk. My temple pulsing, my head fuzzy as if my brain were thick with static cling. It's a very weird thing to wake up when you didn't even realize you were unconscious. Moments before, the queasiness had set in as my dad and I were waiting for a takeout order. I quietly stepped outside for fresh air. I felt dizzy and light headed, and then, BAM! I was down and out.

My dad brought me back to my house. My wife immediately asked what was wrong. She could see the still faint trace of ghostliness on my face. I explained what happened, and then she dragged me by the ear and out the front door to get checked. At first, I refused to go to the ER, so we compromised and stopped in at the local fire station. After a quick diagnostic check, the paramedic on duty highly recommended we proceed to the hospital, just to be safe.

A few days later, I was finally released from the hospital with a clean bill of health after a battery of tests and a lot of prodding and poking. Evidently, I have the heart rate of an elite athlete, which means it is really low. The good news is that at the rate I'm using my heart, it should hold up for another 300 years or so. The bad news is that when your heart beats as slowly as mine does, you're a small dip away from a blackout. It's never happened before, and the doctors said it was possible I'd never experience it again. But

that feeling of opening my eyes and being disoriented with my surroundings—well, that feeling would indeed surface again.

My blackout occurred during an obviously stressful time for me.
I was in the process of a mutually agreed upon exit from a leadership
position in a healthcare startup. I had left a very safe and secure
position with my long-term employer to take a chance at hitting it
big with a small company that was hiring its first marketing execu-
tive. The salary, the equity all sounded great. And it was flattering
because they were recruiting me hard. They really, really wanted me
to join the company. They wanted me! In the end, though, it was
a terrible fit for me, for them, and for everyone involved. I needed
to make a change.

I had been praying about the next chapter of my life for a long
time. But I didn't really like what God was saying to me. I was on
the verge of starting my marketing agency and striking out on my
own. I knew that wasn't what God was calling me to do. He wanted
me to share my story. I wasn't prepared to do that, but I had to do
something. Call it a half-measure attempt.

I'm not sure if the stress of this struggle was directly to blame
for me chasing the sidewalk, but looking back, it makes sense that
possibly I put myself in the hospital because of the burden.

And so I opened my marketing agency. On the first day, I landed
my first client. It wasn't the biggest project ever, but it was more
than adequate to get me going and take away the initial financial
pressure. It was the first of countless clients God would bring my
way. Even though this was a half-measure attempt, God was blessing
it. He had called me to something much more dramatic, but I had
countered with a do-good marketing agency. I was planning to help
a lot of great charities. I was doing God's work, even if I wasn't
completely following God's will. He let me continue. For a while.

Things went really well—extremely well. By the third year of
operation, I had grown the revenue of the company considerably. It

had doubled every year. My take-home pay was nice. I was making more money than I had ever made in my corporate jobs. One year, the revenue I generated placed me in the envied "one percent" in Tennessee. And just as important, I was executing on my business model, to give away marketing services to nonprofits. By the third year of operation, the company had donated more than $250,000 in pro bono marketing services to local charities. The company had also been a finalist three years running in a local award program that recognized the most inspiring up-and-coming businesses in the area. We had been quoted or reported on in media outlets including the *Huffington Post*, *Entrepreneur*, *Forbes*, and *Fast Company*. We were regularly getting inbounds from people who wanted to work for us, from companies who needed help, and from charities who wanted support. And, I was burning both ends against the middle to make everything run. Being an entrepreneur means you wear many hats. It was a lot of stress.

After a while, I resented my job. And when you work for yourself and resent your job, well, that is a great recipe for self-hate if I ever saw one. I also had fallen into my cycle of comparing how I was doing with everyone around me. Other agencies had bigger teams. Other socially responsible companies were really making a difference in the world, not just giving away marketing help to a handful of nonprofits. I couldn't appreciate the small miracles God was fueling me to perform because I could only see the flaws and the shortcomings of what I was doing. I wasn't measuring up. Again!

My shame not only used my missteps and mistakes to amplify the feelings I had of being unworthy, but it also used my strengths against me, causing self-inflicted wounds. I received more damning messages about "not being enough" through my inability to reach those unreasonable goals than I ever did through my childhood trauma and abuse and the series of progressively damaging transgressions, lies, and betrayal that resulted from my inability to deal with my wounds. Basically, my strengths were being used as weaknesses. No matter what I accomplished—success, money, accolades, awards—I never felt like I had really accomplished anything. No matter how many times my wife told me how smart or talented or desirable I was, I never felt loved. The things I was good at, the qualities I could be most proud of, the gifting I'd received from God, all were used to create discontentment, disappointment, and disastrous levels of self-doubt. Anytime I managed to get close to the bar that had been set, it was raised. There was always someone else I could find to compare myself to when I needed to prove that I couldn't measure up. My strengths were the very things I chased around in circles but could never fully capture.

I was absolutely using my business (which I should have used to further bless myself, my family and others) to undermine my life. Because things were going well, because money was coming in, because it was impossible to keep track of my schedule (for me or anyone else), I inadvertently created the perfect scenario to spiral. My erratic calendar had me all over the place, all the time, so I had the freedom to be anywhere I needed to be to follow through with bad decisions. I was the boss, so there was no one to report to if something didn't actually get done. I basically set myself up to fall harder or, more appropriately, to climb higher.

Sin can look like success. You can be falling fast but look like you're climbing. Celebrities show us this truth on a daily basis. Famous, rich, accomplished, by all accounts they have reached the top of the mountain. And then you watch a former NBA standout go on a weekend bender to a brothel and end up in a coma, or a former sitcom star declare himself a "winner" as he shares what's left of his scrambled egg brain with a national broadcast audience.

You witness a much-loved morning television personality's career implode as a result of multiple sexual harassment charges.

There's a fantastic song called "I Took a Pill in Ibiza" that beautifully delivers this truth. Mike Posner sings about the emptiness of success and how different perception and reality can really be. In the last verse of the song, people from his hometown are coming up to him and asking how they can "make it" too, but all he can share with them is a word of caution. He tells them they don't actually want what he has. There's no joy. No contentment. Just a sad, lonely ride without a destination.

We get lost in idolatry and materialism. Power and greed. Self-importance. Self-indulgence. Self-righteousness. Self-medication. As the old adage goes, we climb the ladder but don't realize we have it propped against the wrong wall. We might find "success" or "peace" along the way, but it can come at a price.

When we reach our desolate heights, we are fully engaged in our sin. We have been overcome. We are up to our eyeballs with it. And we are on display, high upon a hill for everyone to see. It's ironic that in some cases, you can reach your lowest low from the highest place around.

You can easily get caught up in satisfying yourself and climb all the way to the top of the mountain, only to arrive at an empty, barren wasteland, miles away from God and what He wants for you—on a desolate height that in actuality is less like a mountain and more like a self-made monument to your own delusional ineptitude. A fortress designed for protection but used to isolate, like Rapunzel in her castle. The problem is you don't have the long hair to throw down so you can be rescued.

But here's the good news. No matter how high up you are, God can reach you. In Isaiah 41:18, God says, "I will open rivers in desolate heights" where there's nothing but barren land and desert. Even there, He can, and will, flow healing waters.

Our God is not a passive God. Even though He's opened the door for a graceful return anytime we choose, He doesn't always just sit there and wait.

Isaiah 42:15–16 says He will lay waste the mountains and the hills. Make the rivers coastlands. Lead the blind by a way they did not know. Make darkness light before them.

Job 16:12, 14 explains:

I was at ease [asleep, numbed, tranced], but He has shattered me. He also has taken me by my neck, and shaken me to pieces.... He breaks me with wound upon wound. He runs at me like a warrior.

Can you visualize God running to you like a warrior? Violently pursuing your heart and tearing limb from limb anything that stands in the way? Not just approaching you, but charging toward you like a rhino? Barreling toward you like a tornado across flat land? Rushing toward you like flood waters? The passionate pursuit of God. Too often, we don't have an appreciation that He is warring on our behalf. Fighting for us. Fighting to get to us. Fighting to wake us up.

It is a fact. When you are far from His will, He will pursue you. And when necessary, He will put a yoke of iron on your neck until you have been destroyed. Breaking you. Wrecking you. Tearing you down in order to build you back up. The remnant, what's left, is a seed of obedience, faith, hope, and love (Deut. 28:47–48).

Our God, however, is patient. He waited patiently as I spiraled. In time, He would use my success, which had ushered me straight to the top of my desolate height, as a tool to heal me. Everything is beautiful in its time (Eccles. 3:11). My desolate height could very well be transformed into a monument of how God moves in the hearts of people.

Whether now or later, God will literally "arrest you" from your sin. In my case, He focused on the "literally" part, but even if your arrest is more symbolic, God will intervene. There will come a time when God's relentless pursuit of you will come to a head, and you will come to a choice. Return to Him, or continue on your climb.

CHAPTER 14

Friday Night Fight

The fight was more of a dispute or rivalry rather than an actual fight, or so I thought. It was just a standoff. A stare-down. That is, until I was picking myself off the parking lot with a swelling, throbbing, bruising right eye.

He was one year older than I was and attended our rival high school. We had both been interested in the same girl, a girl who happened to be a very good friend of mine. As it turns out, he didn't really appreciate her decision to date me. It was a Friday night. In small-town Mississippi, that means you spend the evening bumper to bumper, cruising the strip, trying to impress girls and intimidate guys. Our cruising loop started at McDonald's, went a couple of blocks down, and then took a hard right onto Main Street. You went down about half a mile, made a turnaround out of the Sonic drive-thru, and then headed back to the golden arches to repeat the process. Once you were tired of looking cool with your windows down and your system up, most of the teens would find a parking lot to hang out in. This particular night, a large group of youths had gathered in front of a discount grocery which, over the course of the years, had been the home of many different businesses. Cars were lined up across the entire street in front of the building and down one side. Inside the "L" they formed, there was a small crowd of teenagers just looking for something interesting to do.

My cousin was visiting from out of town and had come with me to hang out this Friday night. He instigated the situation I'm sharing with you now by yelling a profanity at my adversary while driving by the parking lot. Against my better judgment, we circled back and parked just a few cars down and got out. The guy approached us, and my cousin quickly fell back to let me handle my business on my own. We stood there, staring at each other like a pair of boxers at a press conference before the title bout. Other people started to gather. Like sharks in the water, they smelled the possibility of blood. There was nothing better than a Friday night fight.

I was completely convinced that we would stand there, stare each other down, and, after everyone else was bored with the controversy, back away and both save face. It would be a display of how much we didn't like each other, without all the nonsense of getting physically violent.

And then a sucker punch, right to the face. I had looked away momentarily, a cool glance off to the side to let everyone know I wasn't afraid and didn't really even have time for the inconvenience of standing there. That's when he decided we would fight. Bam! I never saw it coming. I hit the ground hard but then rolled over to see him tackling me. We tussled for a moment, and I was able to get on top and apply some leverage, but I couldn't get a clean strike. We both popped up to our feet, and that's when my eye started to throb. He stood there, fists cocked, waiting for me to approach him. I could hear people in the background yelling that I didn't want any more, that I was done. They were right. The pain in my eye was intense, and I didn't really care to make it worse. I could barely see out of it. I hadn't started the fight, but I sure was stopping it.

When I didn't step forward into his personal space, he had the opportunity to declare himself the victor and strut back to his car as if he had accomplished something special. My two choices were to let him gloat or to attack. I let him gloat.

This is the perfect metaphor for how much of my life had played out. My life was a fight, but I just didn't know it—until I got sucker punched. For a while, that punch hurt so much that I really just wanted the throbbing to stop. I couldn't bring myself to fight back. I hadn't been prepared to fight, and I felt as if I had lost before I even knew what was happening.

As I said at the outset, every one of us is in a fight, whether we know it or not. Addicts are well aware of this truth, but many people out there are just hurting too badly to get back up. For some, they are getting punched in the face daily and still don't have a clue how to fight back. Those really in denial just stand there and take the punches, declaring that it doesn't hurt at all.

Of course, there's more to this metaphor. In some cases, we do fight, but we just attack the wrong opponent. Absently throwing punches, we misidentify who the enemy really is.

In his book *The Killing Wind*, Tan Hecheng shares a detailed account of what he calls "a Chinese county's descent into madness during the Cultural Revolution." In August and September of 1967, approximately 100 bloated corpses per hour flowed down the Xiao River through the Chinese county of Daoxian. The bodies were dumped after suffering cruel, painful deaths at the hands of their own countrymen. More than 9,000 people lost their lives during this chaos, which occurred during the Cultural Revolution launched by Mao Zedong to achieve a utopia in China.[1]

Local Communist party officials who feared an insurgency were to blame for the mass killing of villagers who had been branded as "bad elements" for one reason or another. Entire families were murdered to lessen the risk of revenge. This unfathomable activity was perpetuated by fear, hysteria, and atrocious misconceptions about who the enemy really was.

This is an extreme example, but think about this: These people wandered so far from reality that they were convinced they were doing the right thing by attacking their own with agricultural tools and explosives and then sending their dead bodies down the river to rot. They thought the enemy in front of them had to be conquered for their own safety. We are guilty of this same behavior when we blame others for what's wrong inside of us. Let me explain.

In my recovery work, I've done a lot of reflecting on resentment. What I've learned is that I carried a lot of angry, bitter feelings around because of things I had experienced in my life. I had a long list of people who had hurt me, harmed me, let me down, abandoned me, mistreated me, offended me, abused me, misunderstood me, lied to me, manipulated me, burdened me, and intentionally blocked me from what I wanted. People who wanted to see me harmed. To see me fail. To threaten my safety. Some of these resentments were legitimate. Many were not. None of them were worthy of holding on to as I moved through life. All of them were facilitated either through my brokenness or someone else's brokenness.

We all harbor resentments. We look for places to offload the blame and make sense of what is happening to us. We identify people in our lives as adversaries and attribute our wounds to their weapons.

But we aren't wrestling against flesh and blood. The enemy is not of this world (Eph. 6:12). Our real enemy uses seduction, misdirection, brainwashing, distraction, fearmongering, mind alteration, falsehoods, and propaganda until we are snared in our addictions. And when we are caged in our isolation, we're left to throw punches at shadows, fighting adversaries who merely cast darkness on us from a much more powerful force.

The enemy used other people's pain to inflict pain on me. And the pain in me was used to produce suffering (more on that later), all because I didn't clearly understand how to fight. To defend myself, I had to identify and understand where the battle for my heart was being waged, what tactics were being deployed, and precisely how I was being attacked. I had to correctly name my enemy. And then I had to develop tools to fight back, which required a higher power to counter the otherworldly strength of my opponent.

CHAPTER 15

Labyrinth

We walked single file through the pattern, making some small talk but mostly relaxed. We had found the labyrinth by sheer accident while on a break from an intensive group counseling session as part of a weekend retreat—a group of guys who all wrestled with common issues, having all the wrong things in common.

It was my first time in a labyrinth. To be honest, outside of Greek mythology, I had never really been exposed to the concept of a labyrinth. All I could remember is that I thought a labyrinth was where they kept the Minotaur. It didn't sound like a great place to be. But it turns out that a labyrinth can be a very peaceful place, full of meditation, focus, and relaxation. A place of clarity. And within the pathway of the labyrinth that day, I realized something revolutionary.

I've always experienced my life as a very complicated maze. Life felt overwhelming—all the choices to be made, all the paths I could take. I felt confused and astray most of the time, reaching ahead clumsily with my limited sight, fearing what the next turn would bring, worried about a wrong turn or a dead end. I was lost. I thought I needed to solve the maze. There had to be a way out.

It turns out that life is less of a maze and more of a labyrinth—at least for those who believe in God as their higher power and commit to following His plan.

A maze is a complex puzzle that includes choices. It can have multiple entrances and exits and, most importantly, dead ends. A labyrinth, by comparison, offers a single, non-branching path that leads to the center and back out the same way. One entrance. One exit. One pathway.

Psalm 16:11 says, "You will show me *the* path of life" (emphasis added). The world would tell you that every choice you make sets the path for your future. It's a choose-your-adventure kind of life. But God says there is a plan for you, a highly specific plan He has laid out for you.

There's only one path. It twists, and it turns, and sometimes it seems like you aren't going anywhere. Sometimes you can almost see your destination, but the next day, you feel like you are headed in the wrong direction, pressing farther from where you thought you were being called. But if you persevere in the path God has provided, eventually you will enter into the promises He has made. He has ordered our steps. He has carefully crafted the journey He is asking each of us to take. It's not a maze. There aren't dead ends. There might be pain, suffering, trials, tribulations. Bad decisions. Slow to no progress. But it will all be used to advance you to an ultimate end.

When we take things into our own hands, we can paralyze ourselves and convince ourselves that we are trapped in a maze and there's no hope for escape. I spent way too much of my life convinced of that lie. But I no longer waste energy or time worried about the next turn, because I know that the path I'm on leads me to God and His completely perfect will for my life.

I look back at things that happened to me, at failed relationships and poor choices, and I see that I took something very specific away from each one. I see the hard lessons I learned—how important it is to be transparent and show vulnerability, how darkness dramatically magnifies shame, how love isn't something I can ever earn, and how to see the pain in others and have empathy. I've received truths about myself, about others, about life, about love, about God. About my purpose. About my calling.

When you trust that God is in control, the maze of life becomes a labyrinth—and manageable. You quickly begin to see that while the pattern is complicated, curvy, and complex, you indeed have a path. If you are diligent and obedient, this path can lead only to one place. And you'll be so glad you followed it.

But what if you don't feel like you are even on the path? In our ascent to desolate heights, as we stumble about in the dark, as we wander far away, so very far away from God's path for us, it is amazing how easy it is to step back into God's will. I mean, He makes it so very simple. It's laid out for us in Malachi 3:7 where God promises, "Return to Me, and I will return to you." That's it. That's all there is to it.

The reality I had created was one I could not escape. It was the desperation of walking repeatedly into a brick wall and feeling as if I had no way over, around, under, or through it. It was the pain of slamming into it again and again. Feeling trapped. Not realizing I could just turn around. That was me. So even though it's as simple as "return to Me, and I will return to you," it's really not that simple. Not always.

The most ironic part of my story was that when I turned back onto the path of danger, back to that hotel room on the third floor, God was leading me right to Him. He was about to play the role of a surgeon, using a blunt, painful instrument to extract the cancer inside me so I could recover and heal. How incredible is that?

For the longest time, I was headed for the exit—into the wilderness. And the farther away from the center of life's labyrinth I moved, the longer the road back became.

John 12:35 says, "He who walks in darkness does not know where he is going." That was me, literally and figuratively. I was in darkness, flailing. All I had to do was turn around, retrace my steps, and get back on the path that led to God.

That reminds me of the time I went hiking with a stranger. We were deep within the wild, winding around the sides of a mountain with tall trees above, boulders alongside the path, and drop-offs at every turn. My hiking partner claimed to know his way around this particular spot, pointing at the blazes, which clearly marked the various trails. He was supremely confident that he could walk us in and back out of the seemingly endless supply of nature. I did not really know this man. He was on a recovery journey of his own, and we had been introduced briefly through a group meeting. But I trusted his expertise and knowledge of the terrain that surrounded us.

It wasn't long before we were lost. My fearless guide was momentarily confused when he discovered we were not headed in the right direction, which didn't make me feel all that great. After turning in circles and a few false starts, he let out a slight sigh of relief and pointed again at a blaze on a tree just ahead of us. Somehow, we'd missed one of the markers and accidentally trekked down a different trail. We were halfway down the trail by the time we realized it. The only way to get back where we wanted to go was to backtrack until we were at the point where the trail split. The bad news was that we had to retrace our steps, and we lost some time. The good news was that there were clear markers to follow, and we had little trouble correcting our course.

What a powerful analogy for dealing with a painful past, a problematic present, and an uncertain future. Jeremiah 31:21 explains, "Set up signposts, make landmarks; set your heart toward the highway, the way in which you went." God was telling his people to clearly mark the path they took as they were led into captivity, because the way to freedom would require them to return the very way they came. Breadcrumbs, like Hansel and Gretel. Blazes, like the ones marking trees on wooded mountain trails. Leading us back to the labyrinth.

My past was littered with regrets, failures, mistakes, transgressions, betrayals. At some point, I stepped off the path, or simply started walking in the wrong direction, straight toward the exit of the labyrinth. I woke up one day, opened my eyes, and realized I was lost. I wondered how I would find my way back.

I would return one step at a time. I had to retrace my steps. And unfortunately, I had to use the things that created the most pain, shame, and embarrassment as landmarks and guideposts. The only way out is through. To recover from a past we'd rather forget, we must first backtrack and pass by each major misstep to gain understanding, find closure, and connect more of the dots of our story. Our freedom requires us to rediscover the journey that led us to captivity in the first place.

In recovery, that's exactly what I've had to do. The process has required me to revisit some of my most painful memories. I've had to closely study the wounds I received at an early age. I've had to confront my personal demons. I've had to make amends with people I've hurt along the way. I've had to backtrack through all the regrets, all the poor choices, all the ways I've harmed myself, harmed others, or been harmed by others. I've had to be brutally honest with myself about my flaws. I've had to be brutally honest with the people who matter to me.

The only way to get by my past was to go back through it. With every step, I moved closer to the path I was supposed to take, the path that leads forward. At first, it felt like I'd been condemned to wander in a wasteland of regret for the remainder of my existence, but it was a temporary setback in the end.

Once you engage with the past, once you take that first step back, you'll soon feel a change in the ground beneath your feet. There will be a new blaze on the tree in front of you. A different color that signifies you are no longer retracing. A signal that you are stepping out of the past and into the future that God has been waiting to share. And with the understanding of where you came from, you will be better equipped to stay on this path, appreciate it, and make the absolute most of it.

CHAPTER 16

Purgatory

Maybe it would be best if I just took a hard turn into the opposite lane and met that big truck head on. Just give it up. There's a million-dollar life insurance policy to cash, and the source of most of our family's stress and trauma would be removed from the equation. Maybe that would be best.

On this particular day, the enemy was playing a new game with me, feeding me a new and very dangerous lie. I don't think I was actually considering suicide—not seriously. But there was enough merit in the scenario to cause me to at least entertain it, to play it out in my head, to give it mind space, even if just for a few minutes. That's where I was. Months of active fighting, daily battles, doing everything on earth to reclaim my life and finally live for God, with God, and through God. All the work, all the sacrifice, all the pain. No progress. My life still felt as if it were dangling, just hanging by the thinnest of strings. I was sober. I wasn't acting out. But all the momentum and confidence and progress I'd managed in terms of how I viewed myself were slowly eroding. For a moment, my marriage had shown signs of life and improvement, but lately it felt like my wife was revisiting her decision on whether to stay with me or not. Our kids were being kids. Not bad kids. But only parents can understand the strain that little people can put on you, especially when you are in a delicate situation and scratching and clawing for joy.

It was hard. Nothing was settled. After six long months, nothing was really better. It felt like I had spent the last decade in a sin spiral, and now that God had pulled me out of it, what awaited me for the next 10 years was payback, restitution for the wrongs I'd committed, a jail without bars where everyone could judge me, take shots at me (either to my face or behind my back). It felt like purgatory—like I was waiting for life to restart. Frustrating, because I finally knew how to live right and how to seek God and how to stay clear on what's important. I believed that God would not grant all of that insight and then not allow me the opportunity to apply it. I believed that He would finish what He had started. However, that faith was wearing thinner each and every day.

On this Tuesday, I was angry. I yelled at God, even using profanity to punctuate my malcontent. My shouts echoed inside my Toyota Tacoma, the back of my throat feeling as if a cheese grater had been inserted in exchange for my vocal cords. All of this misery, strife, struggle, and wasted time—and then we die? That was my question. What is the (use your own colorful word) point?!

What was happening was easy to explain. Every tool I had in my life for self-medication had been removed. Every coping mechanism I once turned to was no longer available. As a result, I could only sit in the pain and call on God. There was no other way to find relief without taking actions that would further damage me. And I knew that. Emotionally, though, I was in pain. I was tired, and I was hurting.

Satan strikes only in two situations: (1) when you're strong and (2) when you're weak. He takes different approaches based on which state of mind you're in, but he can be very effective in either case. I was feeling weak in this moment. So Satan swung for the fence. "Hey, you could just plow into that truck, set your family up financially, and be done with this nonsense." That was the pitch. On that day.

Not wanting to continue driving in my current state, I pulled into a parking lot, shut off the engine, and retreated to one of my favorite local restaurants. I snuggled into a booth and spread out my laptop and journal on the table.

I began typing frantically to record my emotions, but I was distracted. There was an infant screaming and crying and bleeding tears from her eyes in the next section. A brick wall separated us, but there were large window openings and sound traveled freely. I could hear the wait staff at the front of the restaurant complaining about the child who was disrupting the hip lunchtime vibe the establishment was trying to maintain. The infant's screams were getting louder and more frantic. I looked up to see the mom who had finally stood up and was trying to bounce the baby on her left shoulder. It wasn't working. But then the baby made eye contact with me. And she stopped crying. She stared. I looked back. Made a little funny face. She smiled. The crying had stopped. I was a stranger. But in that moment, I was offering her more comfort than her own mother. It struck me—we were both hurting. That bond is strong. Could she sense my pain? Was she just like every other small child, easily distracted? Did I have food on my face?

I don't know. But in that moment, God showed me that in my pain, because of my pain, I would be able to comfort others, even... *even* when I needed comforting myself in that exact moment.

Acts 2 recounts what happened to the disciples after Jesus appeared to them after His resurrection. He had promised they would receive power when the Holy Spirit came upon them. They were to wait patiently for that to happen.

The passage says that suddenly there came a sound from heaven that filled the entire house where they were sitting. Tongues of fire sat upon each of them. They were filled with the Holy Spirit and began speaking other languages. When the sound occurred, it drew the attention of the multitude, and people were amazed at what they saw and heard. "Look, are not all these who speak Galileans? and how is that we hear, each in our own language in which we were born?" (Acts 2:7–8).

Each of us has a gifting powered by specific trials and specific afflictions that make us who we are. These afflictions, these struggles, create a special language and the ability to speak clearly to others who share our struggle, no matter what that struggle happens to be. In this truth, you can find comfort and a calling.

You can find comfort in the fact that there are people who have walked the road you are on, no matter how dark, rocky, and twisty it might be. There are people out there who get you, who understand what you're going through, who know how your mind works, and who speak your language. You just have to find them. That only requires a step of faith on your part to seek out support groups, raise your hand in church, or just be bold and authentic about what you need with the people already in your life.

You can also find a calling. You were gifted by God, both your strengths and your weakness, your trophies and your trials. All is to be used for His glory. Because of your story, you have the remarkable ability to speak someone else's language. Drugs. Divorce. Abuse. Arrest. Failure. Death. Depression. Sickness. Insecurity. Selfishness. Oh my, this is an endless list. The struggles you are enduring, or have overcome, equip you with a context, a vocabulary, an actual language that allows you to communicate with great effectiveness to others who share your struggle. There is nothing more powerful than that.

The people in Acts 2 were amazed to see men speaking their language, despite their appearance and background, suggesting that shouldn't be possible. Trust me, there are people all around you who share your struggle. They might not look like it. They may appear to have their act together. You'd be surprised where the opportunity for comfort, or calling, can surface.

No matter where you are on your journey, seek out those who speak your language, even if right now you need comfort and can't see yourself responding to a calling. Just the act of helping you will be enormously beneficial to the person comforting you. In any event, please do not sit in isolation with any struggle, big or small. Do not feel shamed by any sin. Do not tell yourself the lie that no one gets you or that no one could really understand. They can. And they don't need a translator. They speak your language. And just as importantly, you speak theirs.

CHAPTER 17

Pain

She looked right through me as she gripped my hands and welcomed me to her session. An elderly white woman was not at all what I had expected to encounter when I stepped into my first experience with qigong. I had no idea what to expect other than what the website had described. It sounded nice enough. Some combination of meditation, breathing techniques, and movement, all aimed at healing while connecting mind, body, and soul.

This gentle, aged lady lingered in our handhold. It was as if she could sense I had entered the building with pain. She gave me a compassionate and concerned look before letting my hands go and explaining the process of her class.

It was awkward, but I tried to clear my mind. I was instructed to bend at the knees, release my arms with my elbows out to the side of my body, my chin pressed in, my back straight, eyes closed, tongue touching the roof of my mouth. I was told to bounce lightly. The next half hour, we were moving energy around our bodies, pushing active energy down below the waist while circulating passive energy above the waist. Don't quote me on that. I may have it backward.

The instructor closed class with a short discussion on pain. I had just spent several hours in a coffee shop mulling over the fact that pain is necessary in healing, that pain is required if we choose to shed light on our problems and commit to God's plan for our lives. It was no coincidence she felt compelled to share the following.

She explained that pain is a sensation. But when the mind gets involved, pain can be transformed into suffering. Pain in many cases is a natural, expected outcome for short-term healing. But the mind creates a chronic problem from it, turning it into something more than it was intended to be.

I do that with pain all the time. I turn it into suffering. I torture myself with it. I make it so much more than it was intended to be.

Often, we pray for God to take the pain away. But think about that for a moment. Is that the right prayer? Hardly ever. Jesus could have prayed that on his way to the cross. But then God's promise wouldn't have been fulfilled. Pain is used very specifically to shape us. We all know the mantra for physical fitness: "No pain no gain!" Yet we don't understand why it might hurt to build spiritual and emotional muscle. We question a plan we don't understand because it's not easy or convenient or painless to follow. It hurts deeply. The pain is not only an unavoidable reality of God's plan; it's a central, mission-critical component in that plan.

God told Paul, "My grace is sufficient for you, for My strength is made perfect in weakness" (2 Cor. 12:9). Paul said, "I take pleasure in infirmities, in reproaches, in needs, in persecutions, in distresses, for Christ's sake. For when I am weak, then I am strong" (2 Cor. 12:10).

Think about the pain required just to bring you to life in the first place. How much more is required for you to live? Why does pain always surprise us and catch us off guard? It is literally a reality from birth.

Kicked back in a torture chamber chair, I waited. The doctor finally came in and explained what would happen next. They would deaden the eyelid with a cream and then a big needle. Then they would pry it open with a clamp, lacerate it, scrape out all the stuff inside, and then cauterize it back together. And I'd be as good as new. Risks would include infection or possibly damaged vision (although that was very rare). She asked me if I wanted to continue with the procedure.

I paused and seriously contemplated saying *No thanks, I'm good. Have a nice day.* But I agreed to proceed. The sty in my eye had proved to be very stubborn. It wasn't going away on its own. The doctor exited while the nurse began to deaden my eyelid. I thought to myself how extravagant the procedure sounded, so invasive, so painful.

I sat for another forever, waiting for the doctor to come back and actually perform the surgery. I almost left the room twice. Dread filled me. I hate things near my eyes. I hate needles. I hate any kind of medical procedure. I hated everything about this. But I stayed. And waited. And finally, the doctor was working on me.

At the end of the visit, I was in pain, bandaged up, looking like I lost a fight in a big way. But the sty was removed. And in a few days, it was supposed to be as good as new.

There have been many moments when I had to choose extreme discomfort and pain to make positive steps and care for myself. I've had to make challenging and hard choices that previously I had avoided at all costs. I've had to purge myself of fears and hurts that I had resigned to live with and deal with forever. Things that, like my sty, weren't incredibly easy to notice. But they were there nonetheless, running in the background and infecting every moment of every day.

My sty surgery was painful. But think about how much more painful "real surgery" is, like when your appendix is taken out or when you have a quadruple bypass. Think about how much more intense the pain of healing has to be when you are extracting something from deep within your body, something that is enmeshed with your organs, in the deepest parts of you. Knotted and twisted. Our wounds aren't skin deep. They aren't cosmetic. They are at our core. There is going to be a lot of pain, and the pain might be long-term. Get ready for it. But there is healing on the other side if you persevere. Let me say clearly, though, you have no pain-free option to pursue. You either engage your wounds, push through the pain, and fulfill your purpose, or you allow those wounds to take over your life. The truth of the matter is that they aren't going away. You aren't going to wake up one day and be rid of them. You aren't going to force them into submission. They will only get worse. They will only cause more and more pain. Until you feel nothing at all.

For a long time, I thought too much about my addiction. And then I thought too little of it. Didn't give it credit for how sinister, pervasive, and cunning it could be. Even in recovery, it was doing its best to wreck my life. To short-circuit my joy. To turn any drop of fear into a tidal wave of anxiety. To set in motion my self-destruction. Any crack, and it was in. Generating thoughts, propaganda, shoving me easily into spirals of shame and emotional loops. When it saw that it couldn't as easily persuade me to act out sexually, it called upon my other idols to take me down.

As I mentioned earlier, there came a time when it was clear that I had placed my family, specifically my wife, as an idol, something that could heal me and make me whole. Something that could take all the pain away. In recovery, I found it difficult to work on my marriage, to try to reconnect with my wife, but at the same time not trigger my addiction.

God has a lot to say about pain, about affliction, about trials and tribulations. I've spent the last several years collecting and arranging passages about pain, why it happens, what it means, and how it should be used. Here's what I've concluded.

Pain is required. We are fallen as human beings. We are fractured from birth. Sometimes, pain is the only way to get our attention and break us down, as I talked about earlier. Lamentations 1:13 says, "From above He has sent fire into my bones, and it overpowered them. . . . He has made me desolate and faint all the day."

Pain is to be expected. 1 Peter 4:12 says we shouldn't consider a "fiery trial" to be something strange happening to us. Don't be surprised when obstacles emerge. If you are working toward God's will for you, trouble will surely come your way.

And when you endure affliction, God rests with you. His glory will be revealed to you. 1 Thessalonians 3:3 explains, "No one should be shaken by these afflictions, for you yourselves know that we are appointed to this."

Pain equips us. We will receive comfort in our tribulation so we can comfort others (2 Cor. 1:3–7). Affliction leads to perseverance, then character, then hope that does not disappoint (Rom. 5:3–5).

Pain is manageable. But it hurts! The Bible tells us we will be hard pressed on every side, yet not crushed; we will be perplexed but not in despair, persecuted but not forsaken, struck down but not destroyed (2 Cor. 4:8–17).

Pain refines us. God has tested us. He has refined us as silver. He brought us into the net, laid affliction on our backs. Caused men to ride over our heads. We went through the fire and the water, but He brought us to "rich fulfillment" in the end (Ps. 66:10, 12). In 2 Corinthians 12:9, Paul says His "strength is made perfect in weakness."

Pain requires patience. James 1:12 (ESV) instructs us to remain "steadfast under trial." Your reward is coming! 1 Peter 5:6–10 promises that after we've suffered a while, we will be made perfect. God will establish, strengthen, and settle us. It doesn't say immediately. It says in "a while" (1 Pet. 5:10).

Pain is temporary. It does come to an end, unlike God's promises that carry on for eternity. Psalm 30:5 explains, "Weeping may endure for a night, but joy comes in the morning." The design is for sorrow to pass through and joy to persist.

The pain will be worth it. In 2 Corinthians 4:17, we read this promise: "For our light affliction, which is but for a moment, is working for us a far more exceeding and eternal weight of glory." The payoff is huge. It says so in Romans 8:18: "For I consider that the sufferings of this present time are not worthy to be compared with the glory which shall be revealed in us."

CHAPTER 18

The Long Tail of Sin

The inside of my head was like dry, cracked dirt. Scorched earth. A wasteland set squarely inside a furnace. My brain felt like it had shriveled and hardened, as if it were dragging against the lining of my skull, scraping off flakes of brain cells as it rattled around, desperately seeking moisture. Each time it made contact, an almost audible panging feeling throbbed the entire upper half of my body.

The house around me was empty, save for a mattress centered in the bonus room, a folding chair in the dining room, and a handful of suitcases and plastic containers with my most valuable possessions wedged inside. In less than a week, I would be driving cross-country with my boys and my dog, leaving behind our long-term community in Nashville. The new destination was Los Angeles, a place I said I'd never live.

I wheeled my eyes to survey the room, making sure the kids hadn't made a run for it. They were in a corner, entertaining themselves with iPhones and iPods. That would buy me at least an hour. My head returned to the pillow on the floor. I felt fortunate that I was no longer hugging the toilet. The night before had ended with dry heaving after I emptied my body of every ounce of food and liquid. This morning's agony was simply the aftermath.

Food poisoning was the likely culprit, either that or an extremely nasty stomach bug. Regardless, I was purging something awful from within me, and soon I would feel like a brand new version of myself.

At this point, 18 months had passed since my awakening, since I had been arrested from my ascent into madness, pulled from the death zone just in time. I had invested in more than 500 hours of counseling, step work, quiet time, group meetings, and other recovery-related activities. I had turned away from the behaviors that previously fed my self-destruction. I had freed myself of chains that previously dragged me down and burdened me daily. I was working hard to tackle character defects that had always prevented me from evolving into the person I was meant to be. There was still much to do, but I was a better man, a better father, a better friend.

Yet here I was, unable to lift my head off a pillow. Lying in an empty room. My brain on the verge of drying out completely and blowing away with the wind. My marriage, gone. My dream home, gone. Almost half of my time with my children, gone. Many of my friends, gone. And now the place I had called home, the place where my kids were born and raised, the place that finally felt comfortable, the place where I was building important new relationships—gone.

My ex-wife was moving to Los Angeles to pursue professional opportunities and get closer to her family. I was left with the choice of being almost 2,000 miles from my boys or packing up my stuff and relocating too. I chose to move. I was convinced that California was not in the best interest of my sons. But without me there, it would be an even worse scenario. So I decided to abandon my life in Nashville, despite the fact that I had built a strong community of support for my journey, made a new house feel like a home for me and the boys, and benevolently stumbled into a very promising connection with someone I believed would play a significant role in my life moving forward. Just when my life was beginning to settle in and possibly make some sense, just when I thought maybe I was being rewarded for my recovery journey, I was being subjected to more consequences.

As frustrating and unfair as it felt, I knew it was all part of the process. A necessary road to travel. MacLaren sums it up well:

> Every sin draws after it as certainly as the shadow follows the substance, evil consequences which work themselves out . . . in the smaller spheres of individual life. . . . The miseries and sufferings which follow our sins are self-inflicted, and for the most part automatic.[1]

In other words, you will reap what you sow. I guess that cliché is true after all. He continues:

> If then we understand the connection between sin and suffering, and the fact that the sorrows which are but the echoes of preceding sins have all a distinctively moral and restorative purpose, we are prepared rightly to estimate how tenderly the God who warns us against our sins by what men call threatenings loves us while He speaks.[2]

His insight reminded me of a television special I saw on ESPN featuring the story of Southern Methodist University (SMU) and its football team's infamous journey from a rising national powerhouse to being wiped off the map by the NCAA's death penalty in 1985. For all the non-sports fans out there, SMU cheated in 100 different ways to build a winning football team, and after several rebukes by the NCAA, its program was effectively destroyed by the harshest punishment in NCAA history. The program is only now showing signs of life, more than 30 years later.

Many of the people who created the cheating culture and conducted most of the illegal and unethical behavior were long gone by the time the NCAA brought down the hammer. The head coach who was there when the ship finally sank wasn't the one who set out on the course toward the iceberg. He just couldn't steer the ship clear in time. That fate had been set in motion and could not be avoided.

This is a great example of the long tail of sin—the echoes that mistakes can make in times to come. The consequence, sometimes delayed, of regrets, wounds, and weakness.

It can seem unfair when the echoes come, when you think you've seen the worst of it—so relieved to have it behind you, whatever *it* is, and to be starting over. But the consequences aren't always immediate. Sometimes your mistakes set into motion a series of other painful events yet to unfold in your life. The tendency, at least for me, is to then ask God what in the world He thinks He's doing. Why is He continuing to punish me for the mistakes I made? Why is some of that punishment delayed? Why now? Why isn't He restoring instead of destroying? Why is He hurting (me, you, others) instead of healing? Why is He not choosing to create a happy ending here? We expect that once we've repented, once we've made amends, once we've given it all up to God, it's time for the miracle, the redemption. That is all true. But if the ship has been set on course toward an iceberg, God makes no promises that you won't still hit it.

Sorrows can be echoes of preceding sins. That's really hard to accept, especially when you feel like you are no longer the person who set the ship on a collision course in the first place. When a changed heart and a revived spirit are within you. When you've begun to transform your life. When you do the work. You likely expect it's now time for restoration, hope, reward, joy. Not the beginning of an even more difficult journey.

Sometimes that is true. And sometimes, the long tail of sin still has to work its way out of the picture. And the tip of that tail is most likely the most painful part of it.

I encourage anyone out there who is trying to change, to rebuild, to make things better, to understand that the echoes won't last forever. At some point, you hit the iceberg, put the pieces back together, and start winning again. It may feel like forever.

But the consequences will work themselves out in your life.

In the midst of the echoes is not the time to give up on your God, even if you are losing what you dearly love. It's exactly the time when He's getting ready to do His most miraculous work. It's not a convenient process. But you can't argue with the conclusion. It's hard. It hurts. I don't know why things are unfolding as they are for you. I can't even begin to answer that question for myself at the moment. But I want to see how the story ends. God tells great stories.

I had to remind myself of that truth as I prepared to leave everyone and everything that mattered to me except these two precious boys and their big fluffy dog. So much loss. So many consequences. And the retribution wasn't over. But neither was my story, or the goodness God had for me.

CHAPTER 19

In a Church Basement

My dad's voice was heavier and more emotionally charged than usual. Than ever.

"Did he ever touch you?" His voice quivered, mixed with a touch of desperation and anticipated anger. "If he did, please tell me. Just tell me the truth."

I sat on the other end of the phone. I pulled it away from my face, rested it on my forehead, then back to speaking position.

"No, he didn't," I finally responded.

It was the truth. He had never touched me. I paused because my father was as close to the truth as he had ever been. There was so much I wanted to share, to confess, in that moment. So many relevant, important things. But I only answered his question, and then I shut down. I just couldn't.

At this point, my dad knew about the arrest, but that was about it. His call was an attempt to put two and two together and make sense of things.

The man he was asking me about was part of our extended family by marriage. He was in his 70s now and had been arrested on charges of sexual abuse involving a minor. By all accounts, it appeared he was guilty.

As a youth, I had spent countless hours in this man's house. He lived two doors down from us. He employed me for several summers, giving me jobs on construction sites. Before that, he offered me odd jobs around his house and welcomed me anytime I wanted to just be there, work or no work. I remember playing his organ. He had a super cool, old-school organ. And I loved music. I would play that organ for hours, having an extreme amount of fun doing it. I remember him sitting a handful of steps away, smiling and watching as I played. Watching with just a little bit too much interest. I thought absolutely nothing of it. Looking back, given the recent developments, it gives me chills.

I can only assume that I was being groomed. That I was in eminent danger each and every time I stepped foot in his house. That I was so fortunate he never approached me. Maybe he was able to manage his sickness during that time. Maybe he was afraid of what my father would do if he found out. Regardless, I was lucky.

If I had experienced abuse at the hands of this man, on the heels of my other childhood experiences, I would have been finished. Snuffed out before I even got started. There is absolutely no way I would have recovered. It was difficult enough for me to overcome what already happened. This man surely would have taken it over the top, to the point of no return.

Fortunately, I was spared from having to deal with this specific experience. I was in the lion's den, many times over. And I was protected.

Still, replaying those experiences as I talked with my dad was traumatic. I could clearly see the pre-teen me, sitting at that organ, playing my heart out while he watched me. It was impossible not to suddenly feel violated, even though no physical boundary had ever been crossed.

I could tell my dad wasn't certain I was telling the truth. He could sense there was more to my story than what he knew about the arrest. He was right about that. Just wrong about it involving this man. I tried to reassure him, because my dad would have done something dramatic if he felt he needed to do something dramatic.

I hung up the phone that day and winced. This was the perfect opportunity to share everything that happened to me as a child. To tell him that while this man didn't harm me, I did experience some things that were harmful, and they had a lasting impact on me. I didn't have the courage that day to tell the truth. Soon, I would share parts of my story. Others would only become apparent as the pages of this book were turned.

A few days after the conversation with my dad, I slipped on a dark gray T-shirt, pulling it down over my face. I caught my reflection in the mirror, the word *triumph* now draped across my chest. How ironic. How far from true. I smirked. No time for God's sense of humor today. I was running late.

I actually just thought I was running late. Instead, I arrived early, the first person to enter the room. It was the basement of a Methodist church, in a room with only one window covered by a drape. The carpet was a dingy medium blue, and badly stained. Traditional high back chairs flanked all four walls, leaving an empty space in the center of the room. The walls were banged, bruised, and largely bare. I sat in the corner, my head in my hands, tapping my left foot as if keeping time to music. My entire left leg was vibrating with a nervous tremor.

After some time alone, an older gentleman entered the room and greeted me. He was like a skinny Santa Claus. Very kind, soft spoken, and authentic. He expressed his gratitude for me coming to the meeting and then retreated to the other corner of the room with a small thermos and what appeared to be a toolbox. He popped open the box, started pulling out laminated cards, and sent one my way across the floor with a flip of his hand. He had a stack of these cards, which provided structure to the support meetings. It was also an easy way to get a newbie talking and integrated into the group.

"Could you read 'the problem' today?" he asked.

I scooped up the card and nodded as I scanned it. There in front of me was my life story, the crux of my crisis, the manifestation of everything wrong inside me. On one laminated page, someone had captured the essence of my illness.

Slowly but surely, the room filled with other men. Some were in athletic gear, others in business attire, some just casual wear. Old, young, tall, short, thin, fat, clean-shaven, and disheveled. A little bit of everything.

There I was, in a room full of men who shared my affliction, who had endured the same wounds, who had made similar mistakes. Men who have walked down the same dark streets as I have. I was surrounded by others waging the same, or at least a similar, war, but it didn't bring peace to me. I didn't experience the feeling of brotherhood. Instead, I immediately sized the room up and put people into categories of how badly messed up they probably were. Again, I thought to myself, *I don't belong here. I don't like what's inside me. The last thing I want is to hang out with other guys who have even more baggage than I do.* I felt unclean just sitting there. Wow, self-righteous. So angry at all the people in my life who, I could already tell, would not be accepting of me and would not be showing me grace. Who would blackmark me and find me unclean and unworthy. And here I was, in a room full of people like me, who all wanted the same things I did, and I was initially unwilling to give it to them.

The meeting started with a check-in. Man after man announced his name and the specific nature of his struggles. Then it was my turn. I took a deep breath and detailed my indiscretions by category. Pornography. Experiences with women and men outside my marriage. Escorts. My arrest. All of it. And then I passed the mic and shrank down into my chair, as the momentary rush of adrenaline I received from shining light on my shadows immediately dissipated, leaving only a fog of shame clinging to my clothes.

You would think I'd gain comfort knowing I wasn't alone, but it hurt worse that there were others out there. Part of the saving grace, I thought, was that I had a unique story and could help others who struggle with feeling unworthy or invisible. My story would be shocking enough to stir in them a hope they had never had. Ha! Turns out I was just an average Joe in a land of broken, damaged people. Not the worst, not the best, just somewhere in the middle. Like everyone else.

But I was missing the point. The fact that my story is common is what makes it powerful. How many people are out there, thinking they are alone, that they are the "only one," and that no one else can understand their struggle?

This room would become a frequent refuge for me during my journey to reclaim my life. I would find men to trust, men who would hold me accountable and support me in my personal growth, men who would go into battle with me, men who would answer the phone at 2:00 a.m. when my mind was racing and it felt like I might self-destruct.

CHAPTER 20

Wife or No Wife

"I don't want to be married anymore."

That's the only phrase I can repeat verbatim, despite what probably was a lengthy conversation. I honestly can't remember. I had been crushed by my worst worldly fear. I had lost her.

I had just returned from a two-week stay in Chattanooga, Tennessee, where I spent my days praying, journaling, attending support meetings, taking meditation classes, and giving my wife some space as she had requested. Upon my return home, we sent the boys to baseball practice with a coach so we could talk.

Sitting at the dining room table we designed together and had built from scratch, a sturdy oak, circular piece with farm house flare to it, we stared at each other in silence. She finally broke the tension by asking how my time away was. After I shared what I'd learned about myself and what I was feeling, it was her turn.

She asked for a divorce.

I went cold on the inside. I wanted to fight it, to convince her it was a huge mistake, but I really couldn't muster up much of anything. I had dreaded hearing those words for a very long time and also told myself that I was making myself crazy, that somehow we'd come through the other side of this trauma.

My mind flashed to the prophetic words of my counselor a few short months earlier. "Stop worrying about whether she is going to leave you," he said with a deadpan stare. "She's already gone. The only question is whether she ever comes back. She probably won't. But she might."

I recalled how the air escaped from my chest, how tears dripped down my cheeks and how I nervously ran a hand through my hair. I was slouched on the couch, opposite his chair. As usual, I had just vomited an overly verbose summary of how I'd been lately and what was going on in my life, and had paused momentarily for him to mop it all up. His words rang true. I saw her every day, some days every hour. Yet she was as far away as she could possibly be. It was as if I was interacting with a remnant of her, a faint lingering abstraction, a trail of particles that hadn't yet burned off in the atmosphere. A shadow. A ghost.

I shook off the memory and stared back across the table at the shadow of the woman who had signed up for better or worse, sickness or health. I started to warm up as resentment and frustration bubbled beneath the surface. I transitioned from shock to outrage. She had endured years of me deteriorating before her eyes. She didn't leave when I had to present an itemized list of transgressions and betrayals to her in a counselor's office. Yet now, after almost a year of healing and health, when I was finally shaking off a lifetime of shame and showing up as the man she thought she married in the first place, it was time to say goodbye, to throw in the towel, to quit. In the heat of that moment, I couldn't empathize with her. I couldn't comprehend that it was hard for her to ask for a divorce. I couldn't accept that maybe too much damage had been done and that this was the best outcome for us. I quickly retreated back to a chilly corner of my mind. My thoughts turned to my boys. My beautiful boys. I had no desire to be a half-time dad. I had no desire to create chaos in their lives because of my past mistakes. But I had no control, no voice in this decision. It wasn't mine to make. Over the coming weeks and months, I would repeat the ebb and flow between extreme sadness and absolute anger. It would take time for the roller-coaster ride to come to a complete stop.

I started writing this book with the outcome of my marriage very much in question. Before I could make it through the first draft, the divorce was long since final.

At first, I thought the point of this work would be to showcase what a miracle God had done in my life by reconciling my relationship with my wife and giving me a happily-ever-after kind of story. But then I realized something. The miracle was occurring independently of my marriage. In recovery, you hear "job or no job, wife or no wife" all the time, meaning that you have to get healthy for you, no matter what happens around you. The commitment to sobriety and well-being has to be nonnegotiable. Saving your life is the priority, and hopefully that comes with rescuing relationships important to you. But regardless, you still have to live, breathe, and exist—job or no job, wife or no wife. The miracle is that God rescued me, not my marriage. That He gave me a chance to be the man He designed me to be. That is true whether or not my wife, or any other person in my life, has the ability to embrace it and proceed in a relationship with me. As it turns out, she didn't.

CHAPTER 21

Mind Games

The mind makes meaning. That's pretty much what it does. It attaches value and interpretation to thoughts, feelings, and experiences. It's a function that's supposed to help us survive, but it can just as effectively crush us and leave us for dead. When dealing with the past, the mind can mislabel things, inappropriately assign judgments and conclusions and definitions. It can make false-positive and false-negative correlations. Memories create a template for how we see ourselves and the future in front of us. Reality is terribly difficult to experience without any bias or slant provided to us by the mind.

For all the wonderful things our mind can do for us, it plays an important role in the creation, internalization, maintenance, and growth of our self-limiting beliefs. It also aids us in generating self-fulfilling prophecies and clouding our reality with worst-case-scenario conspiracies, obsessive thought loops, conclusion-jumping, and future casting.

I spent an inordinate amount of time interpreting any action or feeling, or any absence of action or feeling, as an indictment on my marriage. If my wife wasn't sharing her feelings, she must be planning to leave. If she wasn't able to connect with me, she must only be staying with me because she felt trapped. My imagination could easily roll into storytelling mode whenever fear, hurt, sadness, loneliness, or shame came calling. I could tell myself multiple stories at once, sort of a choose-your-own-adventure style of freaking out. Of course, these stories never had happy endings. They were laced with lies, smothered in shame, and reaffirmed my greatest fears.

The addict within me was eroding my marriage, sabotaging its chance of success, even after I'd pushed everything into the light, even after I'd signed up for a different kind of life, even after I'd committed myself to be the man God intended all along, no matter what the cost. In my addictive, codependent self, the thoughts just kept churning, and that chain reattached to my legs every time I thought I'd shaken it free. I was still spinning.

The mind is also a master of reinforcing what it has determined to be true over time. I bought a white truck recently. It will come as no surprise that once I started driving it, I started to notice tons of other white trucks on the road. Before I purchased the vehicle, it seemed just about every truck on the road was black (the color I thought I was going to select initially). This is a powerful and simplistic example of how the mind bends reality and reinforces truth by filtering your environment. You've likely heard the statistics about the average person being bombarded by 5,000 marketing messages a day. Between advertising, social media, and just the general noise swirling around us, our minds have no choice other than to filter out what seems irrelevant and unimportant, based on what it has determined to be true about our interests and desires. This is a useful feature to get us through the day without breaking down from information overload. The problem is that our minds can function this way as they process and attach meaning, creating truth for us as individuals.

Whatever lies we've been told or that we've told ourselves, if we accept and internalize them, our minds will help us reinforce them over time. Our mind will filter out things that are incongruent with our limiting self-belief and selectively filter through anything that confirms our suspicions about our defects. We start to see what we *want* to see. But of course, it's not as if we actually *want* to think poorly of ourselves.

I told myself a long time ago, subconsciously anyway, that I would be abandoned by anyone in my life who mattered—that I was not worthy of unconditional love from another person. So any friend, lover, or spouse would eventually hurt me and leave me, all because they would get to know the real me and slowly lose desire to be in a relationship.

Over time, my thoughts and, in turn, my actions reinforced this belief, creating evidence that I was absolutely correct. That I was unlovable. That I was not enough. That I would be abandoned. I unknowingly short-circuited countless relationships over the last 30 years, driven by the neediness of this self-limiting belief. My mind would filter information and paint the reality that I was being abandoned, slowly but surely. I'd lean in, grab on, cling to the person. Smothering them. Pushing them away. Or I'd hold them at arm's length and starve the relationship. Freeze it out. In either scenario, as another relationship failed, my mind had another data point to reference and reinforce the belief. It was a vicious cycle. Eventually, it left my heart in pieces and set up a nurturing environment for my addiction.

An article in *Wired* magazine offers another data point for how the mind can continue to dictate your reality long after the truth does. The article focuses on a gene that scientists believe can directly control the amount of pain we experience. In it, the author explains:

Pain is associated with memory-making processes. . . . You don't remember every time you've gone running, but you remember the day you slipped on ice and broke your knee. Pain also leaves an imprint on our cellular memory—the experiences our bodies hold on to and may pass on to our children and grandchildren—which some scientists believe may one day help explain why chronic pain can persist even after an injury has healed. We live with the echo of pain inside us, constantly reminding us to watch our step, back away from the stove, slow down. Someone could get hurt.[1]

This article helped me understand more about how our brains work. And when I substitute *pain* for *trauma* or *abuse* or *wounds*, it feels just as right to me.

After an injury, even the most innocuous things like a pat on the back or a warm bath can send a pain signal to the brain from the site of the injury, serving as a simple trigger to remind the mind of the pain previously created. Our brains become hardwired to process and cope with that pain in specific ways.

In recovery, I had to rewire my brain. What a frustrating exercise! Naïvely, I thought once I had been enlightened I would magically overcome all my defects and issues. What I learned was that knowledge alone wouldn't get me very far. I had to apply it. That meant helping my brain process information differently. That meant practice, perseverance, and some additional pain. That meant months of hard work to short-circuit old thought patterns and replace them with healthier, more productive ones.

In his book *Redemption*, Mike Wilkerson, offers a great example of the journey required for healing. He talks about the Israelites who had escaped Egyptian captivity but were lost in the wilderness. They were "already free from slavery, but they were not yet home."[2] It was only the beginning of their story. Even though they had been removed from an evil oppressor, they weren't pain-free. "They still carried their old wounds on their backs, and the wilderness held its own new troubles."[3]

In my story, this was a troubling realization. Just because I had been granted a clean slate didn't mean it wouldn't be complicated.

Just because I had a new opportunity in front of me didn't mean there would be an absence of obstacles. An awakening is never without adversity. In fact, it is usually required. I was an animal trapped for decades and suddenly freed from its cage. Back in the wild. Trying to figure out how to survive. Hoping my natural instincts for survival would kick in before it was too late. Realizing that my natural instincts were largely to blame for my predicament and that they needed to be honed and improved, if not largely re-engineered.

I saw a video once that illustrates this process very well. It featured an engineer named Destin Sandlin who conducted an interesting experiment using a backwards bicycle. A welder friend of Sandlin's tweaked a bicycle's steering so when you turned the handlebars to the left, the wheel turns right, and when you steered right, the wheels cut left. Sandlin thought he would master this backwards bicycle in a matter of minutes. It took him eight months to ride it successfully. It was a daily exercise to overcome his brain's cognitive bias of steer left to go left. He had to rewire his brain before he could ride the backwards bike.[4]

Sandlin has appeared before countless audiences in recent years, challenging crowds to try to ride the bike. It's the same story every time. Some overly confident audience member saunters onto the stage, mounts the bike, and can barely advance two feet before losing control and toppling over. No one can ride it on the first, second, or even third try.

But the most interesting part of the story is that Sandlin asked his six-year old son to see if he could ride the bike. He couldn't at first. But only two weeks later, the kiddo had mastered it. That isn't a surprising outcome, because as we age, our habits and biases are more deeply embedded and harder to override.

This is the point I missed for the longest time. Sandlin knew that when riding the backwards bike, he needed to turn the handlebars to the right to steer to the left. He had the information, the instructions. But his brain was so strongly trained to steer right to go right, it took months to divert his thinking into a new path, one that was counterintuitive. On the day of my arrest, I was revived. I opened my eyes for the first time in forever, and I immediately wanted everything about my life to be different. I wanted to start living as the best possible version of me. But I had been wired to believe the lies. I had deeply embedded habits undermining me. I had character defects I had long since perfected. It would take time to rewire. I needed to be patient. I needed to anticipate the games my mind would play on me. I had to stay the course. I had to keep turning right when I wanted to go left until it felt natural, until I mastered a new, improved, and "backward" way of thinking.

Here's a specific example of what that looks like for me. There have been many days when I wanted to give up during this process. Many days when I didn't see the point, when it felt like an absolute, complete, utter waste of my time and energy. I remember one day in particular. I woke up, alone in my home. Called my sponsor. I was working through my resentments, fears, and character defects as homework. I thought I might get a "good job" from him, but instead, I hung up the phone feeling beaten down and discouraged. He questioned whether I had fully articulated my defects. He suggested there were several important people missing from my list of resentments. He told me I still needed to do a lot of work and chuckled when I balked at the idea that I needed to dig more deeply. Once again, my thought patterns, my feelings, my response to my feelings, all had been critiqued and criticized. I planned to send him a respectful email thanking him for his support and letting him know I was done with this process. I didn't need a daily reminder of how insufficient and incompetent I was. I didn't need someone second-guessing me and causing me to have zero confidence in even the simplest of decisions. I didn't need to be shamed further for my defects. None of this was what I needed.

Looking back on those emotions, it's obvious that the wounds, the lies I'd been fighting, were still alive and kicking. They were fueling a lot of how I was interpreting life in that moment. I remember pausing and engaging in quiet time, asking for some divine intervention and perspective. I felt entirely off and dejected and low on hope. And I didn't like the way it felt. I was still driving my bike the old way.

One thing led to another during my quiet time, and I ended up on YouTube watching a few videos on meditation. And then a "random" video showed up. I placed quotes around the word *random* because obviously I was intended to watch it. The video was a commencement speech given to graduates at the University of Texas in 2014. Naval Admiral William H. McRaven was the speaker. He laid out wisdom gleaned from nearly 40 years of service, including lessons learned during his Navy Seal training.

About halfway through his speech, he told a story about uniform inspections. Students would try their best to get their uniforms perfectly starched and pressed, their shoes polished. No matter how hard the students tried, the instructors would always find something wrong with their uniforms. Failing a uniform inspection resulted in the instructor ordering you to run down to the beach and roll around until you were covered in sand. Then you had to stay in that uniform for the remainder of the day, cold, wet, and sandy. The admiral shared how some students just couldn't deal with the fact that no matter how hard they tried, their efforts were unappreciated. Those students quit. They never completed the training. According to McRaven, they didn't understand the purpose of the drill. The instructors were not going to allow a perfect uniform. That wasn't the point.[5]

I was still trying to perform, trying to be the most emotionally healthy and balanced person on the planet. To get all the answers right. To feel like I had made it and thus had good reason to no longer feel shame or fear or guilt or any of those emotions. That's not the point.

It was another lesson. Another opportunity to change my perspective and to think about situations in my life differently. In the past, I would have just missed the point. I would have quit on my sponsor. And I would have missed the opportunity to improve myself. But this time, I climbed back on that damn bicycle and tried again.

CHAPTER 22

Cracker Barrel

My eggs were hardening. The last few fingers of steam were fading from the top of my white, porcelain cup of coffee. I hadn't stopped talking for at least 10 minutes. I was pouring out my entire story at that table.

"Stop, just for a minute," he said. "Eat your food. It's getting cold. And just listen. I can see you have some shame about what you're telling me. I want to make you feel comfortable sharing. So eat."

I scooped a fork full of scrambled eggs and slowly lifted them to my mouth, tears trickling down both cheeks. I wiped them away as I slid the food in, drawing a sip of coffee before returning fork to plate for another bite. I was famished, and the emotion required to share what I was sharing had drained what little energy I had left.

He leaned in slightly as he began to speak. He was one of the most godly men I'd ever met. Over 30 years of ministry. He had positively affected so many lives. I had come to appreciate his wisdom, his direct line to God. He absolutely had that type of connection. It was important to me that this man knew who I really was. Our initial introduction, our ongoing relationship, and every interaction we'd ever had were all carefully orchestrated by God. All leading up to this Cracker Barrel breakfast.

He looked at me without flinching, without blinking. Staring into my eyes. I expected him to tell me that God loved me despite all that had been done to me and all I had done to myself and others. I expected him to say that God had a purpose in my life. That God had forgiven me and that I was renewed in Him. He did say all of that. But first he told me about being taken advantage of sexually by his teenage uncle and how that threw his life out of control until he was in his 30s and several years into marriage. He shared many of my transgressions and regrets. He shared many of my wounds. He had walked the road I walked. The most unlikely person in my life identified in a personal way with my story. It was remarkable.

After he finished his story and asked a few additional questions about mine, we exited the restaurant and sat in my truck. He prayed over me, a very powerful, inspired prayer. Halfway through, he transitioned from English into a language I didn't recognize. I have no idea what he was saying or praying. All I know is that as he spoke in a foreign tongue, I started weeping profusely and felt affected all the way to my core. When he switched back to my native tongue, he was no longer speaking to God, but to Satan. And he said something so powerful, so compelling, that I pretty much remember it verbatim. He said, "You thought you had him right where you wanted him. Alone. Weak. In the dark. Defeated. But all you did was pour gas on the fire. All you accomplished was making his resolve all that much stronger, fueling what God had ordained for his life. You propelled him into the light. And God is using all of it to glorify His kingdom, to bring about His will. To strengthen this man for wonderful things."

As the man left my truck, I felt God was still sitting in the passenger's seat. The air was heavy. Thick, warm, covering. I didn't feel alone, for the first time in a long time. I turned the key in the ignition and turned away from another layer of shame that previously had stalled my progress.

And I drove away with a powerful vision of God using all of Satan's best work to pressure test and prepare me for what He wanted for my life.

Why did you make me this way?

What an important question. *Why me?* is another variation of it. Anyone who has experienced pain, who looked around one day and discovered they were standing atop a desolate height, anyone who isn't happy with how life has turned out so far—this is a question we ask over and over again.

Romans 9:20 reads, "Will the thing formed say to him who formed it, 'Why have you made me like this?'"

Of course it will! Of course we will! It's a normal human response to ask this question. The question itself is actually not bad, but the intent behind it is really what we have to understand. The implied meaning of the question is to assume something is wrong with the way you've been made. The *why* is accusatory, suggesting we would have done something different. Instead, we should ask the question to learn the powerful truth of *why* we were specifically crafted by God in this way—to receive the truth about what our story really means, and what God will do with it.

It's okay to be curious about what God is forming, what He is making out of your life. As long as you don't want to weigh in with a better, more convenient, more appealing plan. Until we accept what He has for us, all of it, good and bad, we won't be able to step forward in His will. We won't see the promises in our lives fulfilled. Job 33:12–13 says that God is greater than man. And then the question comes back at us, "Why do you contend with Him?"

My pastor friend was burdened with experiences, trials, and tribulations, and God made use of them. I have also been burdened with specific afflictions, and I feel led to use them as well. Luke 12:48 explains that "to whom much is given, from him much will be required."

I don't say that to suggest I am special. In fact, the Bible says that not many wise or mighty or noble are called (1 Cor. 1:26), which means God is specifically interested in using people like you and me. People who have regrets as long as the day, transgressions as dark as the night, and pain in excess. We are the ones called to save this world. Somewhere along the way, I saw a quote that said those with the deepest scars have the strongest hearts. They also are the most beautiful reflections of God's grace. If that's you, know that He is going to do great things through your circumstances. If you allow Him to work in your life. If you engage with your story.

What do I mean by your story? Great question. Keep reading!

CHAPTER 23

Grasping the Wind

I couldn't believe it. I was ashamed. But it was true. I was jealous of this precious baby. The baby I helped bring into the world. What kind of monster was I? Shame swept across me, invading every pore as I realized the feelings bubbling inside of me. Let me clarify something. I love my kids (more on that in an upcoming chapter). But the birth of my first son created some very confusing emotions. It can be hard for a dad to bond with a baby, in the very beginning at least. The child is 100 percent dependent on the mother, for food, comfort, pretty much everything. Dad has to wait his turn to receive much in the way of affirmation that he needs. I felt left out of the equation for the first several months of parenthood. I also was no longer the priority, my wife's sole focus. I felt isolated and alone.

A healthy person could probably assess these feelings, understand that they are quite likely normal, and let them pass by, largely avoiding any lingering effects. But I wasn't healthy. I was hurting. I needed things I didn't even realize I needed.

As time went on, I eventually bonded with my son and was able to have all the wonderful emotions and experiences I had anticipated being part of fatherhood. But with my wife, a fracture had occurred.

Pornography was losing some of its power over me. It had become a habit during the early years of my marriage, but now I needed a more tangible outlet. The transition started out harmless enough.

Chat rooms, Internet postings. Just electronic exchanges. Eventually, the stimulation I received from these interactions rang hollow. On a business trip to Florida, I made a rather ominous decision after a few drinks with coworkers, and I crossed a line that couldn't be uncrossed. I contacted an escort through the Yellow Pages.

After she left my hotel room, I remember calling my wife with tears running down my face. I'm not even sure what, if anything, happened, but I was overwhelmed with shame. I couldn't tell her what was wrong. I just sobbed and babbled on incoherently with a mix of alcohol and regret scrambling my brain. That night was the beginning of a disastrous decade. It opened a door that was not easily closed, and it planted a seed of doubt in my wife that ultimately would undo everything.

That night is when she began to pull away, physically and emotionally. I'm not sure which occurred first, but that doesn't really matter. A wall had been erected between us. I sensed she was going to abandon me like everyone else had, so I pressed in and was needy. I smothered her. I longed for her to fix me, to tell me I was loved no matter what. But I couldn't share the "no matter what" that I wanted to be loved in spite of. As things slowly spiraled, I began seeking affirmation from external sources. Interactions with other anonymous men and women I met online. Visits to massage parlors, and a few calls to escorts. And then, I had a short-lived affair. I was searching. I was seeking. I wanted intimacy and connection. I wanted to feel affirmed. My brain had been wired to believe that sexualized experiences were the answer. With each encounter, I became more aware that what I was reaching out to grasp was little more than wind. But I kept wrapping my fingers around it, trying to capture it in my clutches. With every transgression, the shame was magnified. The isolation grew more pronounced. The need to perform in other areas of my life grew exponentially. The emotions rumbled within me. I was an unhappy man with a short fuse. The worst possible version of myself. I wanted a do-over. But I didn't even understand what was happening, why I was doing any of it, or how to stop it. And I didn't see any way out, or down, so I just went further up the mountain. Hoping to find distraction from the wreckage of my heart. Hoping to not feel anything at all.

CHAPTER 24

Story

Imagine a box full of puzzle pieces. Let's say that somewhere along the way, you found this puzzle in the attic. No box top. You have no idea what it is supposed to look like upon completion. Just a box full of pieces. Lots of tiny pieces.

For all we know, all the pieces aren't even there. You just stumbled upon this puzzle. But if you get curious enough to build it, to start putting pieces together, the picture will gradually emerge. At first, it's slow going. Patience is required. You make a border to at least frame the work that needs to be done inside. You start making connections, sometimes just one piece with another single piece. Sometimes multiple pieces start to merge, and eventually sections of the puzzle come together. You start to see bigger relationships, and you get a glimpse of what the big picture might actually be. If you work long enough, bridges will form across multiple sections, and collections of pieces will form surprising relationships with other collections of pieces. You can take a good guess at what the final product will look like, though there are still elements of it that remain in doubt. Eventually, you complete the puzzle. Most likely a few pieces are missing. Most likely there are a few pieces that have broken ends and somehow don't seem to fit anywhere. But you have enough of the puzzle together to see what the top of the box would have shown you. You can see it, all of it, the pieces working together. When you show it to others, they can see it, too.

This is usually where we first find our story. It's busted up into a thousand tiny pieces, stuffed in a box without any clues as to what all the pieces might make when assembled. In my case, I walked around with this box of puzzle pieces for years, even decades. It never even crossed my mind to sit down and put them all together to see what kind of picture they would create.

Dan Allender, renowned author and founder of The Allender Center, teaches, "Healing comes when our story is raw, bone-deep and full of hunger for what only Jesus can offer." As a result, he pleads that we "take seriously the story that God has given you to live. It's time to read your own life, because your story is the one that could set us all ablaze."[1]

In his writing, Allender expresses the belief that while God wants us to "relieve suffering, pursue justice, facilitate reconciliation and free the heart to love,"[2] He desires us to do that in a way that reveals His character. Allender says we must show our uniqueness to the world as we heal it so that we "reveal the vast creativity of a God who loves to bring change through the most unlikely channels."[3] In other words, our story is just as important as the deeds we do. Have you ever seen an exposé on an accomplished athlete who had to overcome something challenging to get where he or she is today? Maybe a brush with the law, an abusive or oppressive childhood, a physical disability, or a family tragedy. Learning about where they came from, what they overcame, creates a new level of admiration and respect in you.

God's miracle in your life isn't just what you give back to the world, or the change you create, or the difference you make. The miracle is that He used you to do it, despite all your shortcomings, your shame, your deficits, your weaknesses. He used you. Despite all that's so very much wrong with you.

Your story unlocks that power. It defines who you are. It helps you understand where you came from and why you're here. It's important, both for your healing and for helping others.

In his book *Strangers to Ourselves*, Timothy Wilson urges us to stop minutely studying every feeling and instead put it in perspective of a longer life story.[4]

I was stuck staring at individual puzzle pieces and agonizing over not knowing what to do with them. I saw myself in a thousand cuts, scattered and fractured and without rhyme or reason. I was obsessing over every feeling and failing to see my life in the context of a narrative. The story. All of the individual pieces made no sense until they were connected. I needed context. I needed the bigger picture. I needed perspective.

So one day, I finally started solving the puzzle and finding the top of my box.

In her book *Stiches*, author Anne Lamott shares a metaphor similar to my previous visual of a puzzle. When talking about the past and healing, she says:

> You start wherever you can. You see a great need, so you thread a needle, you tie a knot in your thread. You find one place in the cloth through which to take one stitch, one simple stitch, nothing fancy, just one that's strong and true.[5]

After a while, you attach one section of cloth to another until you have a tapestry that presents context, meaning—story.

You would assume it was easy for me to draw a straight line from my early experiences to my eventual indiscretions, from my adolescent trauma to my adult addiction, from unmet needs in childhood to the shame and inadequacy I felt as a grownup. But it wasn't. In fact, decades passed without any thought that such a link existed. As men tend to do, I had compartmentalized all the individual pieces of my story, just like my father used to insist that none of the various foods on his plate touch each other. As a result, I had no way of understanding how I was wired, why I made specific decisions, why I carried specific feelings, and what was really happening inside of me.

I also had a terrible case of repression. Malcolm Owen Slavin and Daniel Kriegman, a pair of renowned psychoanalysts, suggest:

> Repression allows the reality of the true self to be put out of consciousness and to be held in reserve so that it can be allowed to re-enter the child's repertoire when conditions change and the need for repression is lessened and can be retrieved, as the child's true self is needed to fulfill his or her unique interest and destiny.[6]

That's what the day of the arrest did for me. It was time for my true self to be needed. It was time to fulfill my unique destiny. It was time for me to start putting the pieces of my life back together until I could see my story, until I could stitch my past experiences together and gain a clear picture of who I was, where I came from, and what I needed to do next.

It connected the dots for me. The experiences I had with other men had nothing to do with my being confused about my sexual preference. They had everything to do with me needing to reconcile what happened to me as a child. They were a misguided attempt for me to make sense and to close the book on those early interactions. I was trying to process that shame, deep in my subconscious. And because I didn't understand what was happening and why, it just created more shame for me to manage.

My parents unintentionally engrained an unhealthy desire to perform, to accomplish, to achieve, to be recognized. Couple that with low self-esteem, and it's not surprising I would be perpetually chasing a carrot always just out of reach. Abandonment was my greatest fear, affirmation my biggest need. In my marriage, I set up a scenario in which affirmation was being withheld, and abandonment was all but a guarantee as soon as the secrets came out. The fact that this would cause me to retreat further, to isolate, to medicate, and to lose more of myself doesn't excuse my behavior, but it surely helps explain it.

That's what is so critically important about your story. It makes sense of the nonsense. It clears out the clutter, short-circuits all the confusion. It provides a view into cause-and-effect relationships. I don't use my story as a way to justify or excuse any of my decisions or actions. I do use it as a way to analyze, decipher, explain, and understand how I got from base camp to my desolate height. When I look back on the path that led me astray and put all the pieces of that puzzle together, my past not only helps me see clearly why I ended up where I did, but it also provides everything I need to make sure I never go there again.

It's not like every single memory or choice fits clearly into the puzzle of my story. It's not like I don't still have questions for myself and for God. There are things I can neither define nor defend. You'll experience the same. There will be loose ends. But if you do the work to connect the dots, you will find clarity.

CHAPTER 25

Avatars

My fingers slowed as the inspiration drained from my pores, the way air exits a balloon as it is being manually emptied. I was out of creative juice. I had been hacking away at a novel for months but had only about 15 pages to show for the time spent. It seemed inevitable. The novel was destined to join the graveyard of half-completed manuscripts cluttering my desktop. At least it was dying a quicker, less painful death. I had labored on other works for years before the plug was finally pulled.

The title of this book was *Hookers and Jesus*. It was a fictional story of a young man and his crusade to save prostitutes from their lives on the streets as he searched for his sister, who had disappeared years before after becoming a victim of sex trafficking.

Yes, I was writing a novel about a guy trying to save prostitutes. While being arrested for visiting one. This is as clear a picture as I can draw about the conflict and the duality within me.

Reprehensible. Unforgiveable. Shocking. Disgusting. Despicable. Just a few of the adjectives used to describe my past actions. People have spoken each of these words directly to me, so it is safe to assume that they've used other descriptors in my absence. I try not to think about that too much. Sure, there are people who don't think it's a big deal, and others who want to understand what drove me to that place, because they know there is more to the story. But most people...

One easy way for people to process the facts about my past is to write me off as a hypocrite, especially since I'm a practicing Christian. It is absolutely true that my actions and my beliefs were not aligned, that I was lying about who I was and in denial about what I needed. But I don't view it as hypocrisy in the least.

I'm not gearing up to defend myself here, or play the victim, or blame others, or minimize my mistakes in any way. But it is important for you to understand how to reconcile my story without using the flimsy stereotype of a hypocritical Christian.

Those of faith tend to place immense pressure on themselves to be perfect so they can protect their ability to witness to others. They sit quietly in pews on Sundays and smile as they wrestle with their secret sins. Those not of faith typically carry the misconception that believers don't have to engage in the hand-to-hand combat of the human condition and its daily depravity and have no way to understand or empathize with someone who doesn't have all the Sunday School answers to life.

In our society, there is a subtle and foundational lie that has infiltrated most of our lives. We are made to believe that we are the only one struggling. I know now that many others can relate to what was spinning inside of me. But that insight came way too late for me.

As I struggled, I compartmentalized and managed. I crafted my image. I projected and performed. I tried not to show vulnerabilities or weaknesses, and I didn't address my wounds. Along the way, I created an internal split that only grew wider over time. With part of me isolated and far removed from everyone else, and the other part furiously and tirelessly performing to compensate for the part in hiding, I searched the eyes of others to see if maybe they were hiding as well. But they were good at hiding, just as good as I was. I saw only the performance, the mask they held in front of themselves to shield the world from the person inside. Unless someone was unlucky enough to have been branded for a mistake or exposed as a fraud. And then I witnessed how others reacted and was further convinced that I could never let anyone know how defective I was. No matter what.

The process was subtle, like the gradual pull of the ocean that deposits you far down the coastline as you float. Suddenly, after a long and imperceptible series of micro-movements and experiences, I had drifted. I found myself alone, and in danger.

My younger son and I were talking through hypothetical scenarios over breakfast one morning. Really important, world-changing topics like who would win in a fight: a crocodile or a shark? As it turns out, we weren't the only ones posing these types of questions. After a brief discussion, we turned to the Internet and quickly found a message string with people debating an improbable battle between a salt water crocodile and a great white shark. I don't know that we received guidance from anyone who was actually an expert, but most of the dialogue seemed plausible and sensible enough to me. I'll boil it down to this. The consensus was that the great white shark would be too powerful and deadly for the crocodile if they were to meet in the deep waters. However, if the shark found itself in shallow water, a natural habitat for the crocodile, the odds would swing in favor of the croc. Out of its environment, away from the space in which it was designed to swim, the shark would lose its advantage and place itself in a precarious position.

In my story, I was the great white shark—lured from my base of strength into a darkness, led to thin air where my strength was transformed to weakness, where my reflexes were slowed. I was in enemy territory, and the enemy intended to kill me.

I had become disoriented by the false hope of idols, blinded by the quickly fading beauty of addiction. I was out of control, and with each passing day, the vices I turned to produced less comfort but continued to add to the combustible vat of emotions I was suppressing, heaping on additional guilt and hurt and anger and sadness. I didn't know what else to do other than up the medication, take a bigger dose, a larger hit, a more dangerous risk. More and more and more. And it was never enough, not for long.

All of these variables mixed together into a deadly concoction, a monstrous shadow that enveloped me, that followed me around from the inside, that colored everything I thought, felt, said, or did. It continued to take more of me, reducing my true self little by little, creating a numbed hopelessness where the light gradually dimmed in my eyes and my soul. I was a zombie. Marching upward. Tranced. Hypnotized. Responding to a gravitational pull that was so much stronger than I was. Left to wage my emotional wars far from my natural environment and base of strength.

Through this process, I developed a lot in common with the Bradford pear tree. Gorgeous with its big white blooms, a puffed-up demonstration of nature. Used as ornaments in front yards across the country. Yet despite the alluring beauty, Bradford pear trees are filled with empty promises. They have the weakest branch structure of any tree and also short life-spans. They literally bust themselves apart at the seams. They are not as magnanimous as they first appear. Even more damning for the beautiful Bradford is that although it was thought to be a sterile tree when introduced to the landscape, it actually can, and does, cross-pollinate with other pear trees.

Because of this cross-pollination, pear trees have spread wildly across our environment. And the offspring that Bradfords help birth actually revert to a form of tree known for its thorny thickets that choke out other types of trees. Bradfords are an environmental eyesore, a cancer.[1]

I share all of that to say this. Bradfords are just like our idols and addictions, which always promise to cure what ails us. They are attractive. They offer us what we think we really need. But they are full of empty promises. The Bradfords are just like us addicts, as we put on our masks and tell the world we're okay. In the end, we are hollow. A façade. Potentially toxic. Those who will "perish in their own corruption" (2 Pet. 2:12).

The outside world only gets glimpses of the tragic pain that lurks inside. They only see a hologram when they look at us, a well-constructed mask, an avatar that has been designed specifically to project what we think they will approve and accept. There's no way they could handle what is churning within, no way they could accept the shadow. We now identify with the shadow. There's no turning back. That's what our mind has created as reality for us.

In my experience, I lived with two masks: the person I wanted people to believe I was (the performer) and the miserable person who emerged when no one was looking (the offender). The performer could never generate enough success and achievement to match the shame produced by the offender. With every misstep the performer made, with every mistake the offender made, the cycle just continued to spin, round and round, faster and faster. The wounds, the unmet needs, the untapped emotions just continued to intensify.

Neither of those men were actually me. The performer and the offender were both shadows cast by my true self. They were both avatars. One a lie for the outside world. One a lie for my internal world. Neither was true. Yet, both dictated my truth.

I've forced myself to take a balanced view in order to bridge the gap between these two inaccurate and incomplete parts of me. I see it as a fence separating two unhealthy fields of emotions. On one side of the fence, you wallow in shame and guilt for your past mistakes, taking on *unworthy* and *unforgiven* as the terms used to define you. Forever unclean. The other side of the fence is characterized by an inability to take responsibility. On that side, you play the blame game. The world is out to get you. Bad things happened to you. Choice was taken from you. You are the victim, and God is unfair. The trick is to balance and walk along the fence, trying not to fall on either side. Because the truth is that bad things did happen to you. Some things about your life truly seem unfair. It's not all your fault. And you didn't respond perfectly to your circumstances. Maybe you responded very poorly to them. You compounded one mistake with two, and two with more. You need to have a degree of guilt stirring along with regret and remorse. But your past and how you responded to it are just pieces and parts of your story. Don't allow yourself to be defined by them.

To heal, I had to accept my truth. The things I desired were good. The wounds I had were deep and real. I was overwhelmed by shame and fear. I was attempting to process my past (a necessary exercise) without healthy coping mechanisms or tools to approach it effectively. And I employed terrible judgment. I allowed defects in my character to override my conscience. I lacked faith. I chose comfort over courage. I hurt others and myself. I lost my way and continued to make things worse by struggling instead of making things better by surrendering.

Accepting both sides of the truth allowed me to retreat more rapidly from my desolate height. And step by step, I was able to move closer to my base of strength where I was designed to fight and win. It allowed me to reconcile the competing parts of myself and finally silence the noise of dissonance and confusion that rattled around inside of me. It allowed me to step out of the shadows and set down my masks. Ultimately, it also has given me more empathy for others who are standing atop their own desolate heights. I know exactly how they got there. And just as importantly, I know what it will take for them to climb back down.

CHAPTER 26

Parenting

Her dad is sitting at the opposite side of a long, wooden table in the back corner of the restaurant. Slacks and a blue shirt, standard corporate issue. He quietly rages at the little girl while her mom sits beside her, oblivious or just uninterested in what is happening. The family is evidently in a hurry to get to their next destination, as they quickly eat their dinner. Everyone, except the girl.

The dad's restless knee is banging up and down beneath the table, almost connecting with the underside of the top with each vibration. After a few minutes, the girl sprawls along the bench. She alternates between sitting and lying down and standing, wallowing around like little ones do. Her dad is progressively agitated with her. His face gives him away. He toggles between disapproving glances in her direction and absentmindedly checking his phone. There is no eye contact with his daughter or his wife.

His agitated hands cut across the front of his face after saying for the third time, "I told you to eat!" The little girl shrinks. She stops wallowing, sits straight up, and carefully places a piece of broccoli in her mouth, chewing slowly as she looks at the floor, her shoulders slumped, her face long. Dad is back to his phone now, his leg going a mile a minute, his frown deepening the crease across his forehead.

As I watched this family interact, I was saddened. For the girl. For the dad. For the mom. For myself. For my boys. There was a time in my life when I was not always present, even when I technically was there. I have no way of knowing what this guy was really like, or what he was really struggling with that night. Maybe he was lost in addiction. Maybe he was just a jerk. Maybe he was just having a bad day. Who knows? What I do know is that it was an out-of-body experience for me. I could see myself. From the clothes, to the impatience, to the mindless phone usage, to the banging knee beneath the table, to the twisted face that only spit out disdain and contempt and discontent.

To this point, I haven't said much about my boys. I find it difficult to write about them. Uncomfortable. Don't let their omission from this story suggest that they aren't a very significant part of my life. I was able to largely protect my ability to be a good dad even as I was disintegrating in every other aspect of my life. My role as a father was the last part of me to be impacted by my sickness. For years, I compartmentalized my relationship with my sons in a positive way, shielding them from having to endure any negative consequences from my poor decisions. I spent time with them. I invested in them. I loved on them. I tried to be the very best father possible. They were loved by me as deeply as I could love. I wanted them to think I hung the moon. In the year leading up to the arrest, though, the darkness cast its shadow over my relationship with my kids as well. I was less patient. I was less present. My daily interactions began to look more like the dad in the restaurant. The light inside me was fading, and I'm pretty sure they could sense the shift taking place.

The arrest snapped me to attention. But I was not able to protect my boys from the repercussions of my brokenness. During that first year after my arrest, at the ages of 10 and 8, they had to hear about how Dad had made mistakes. They had to make sense of Dad sleeping on the couch or upstairs in his office. They had to take a back seat to my marriage while I pressed and pushed and tried everything I could to repair that relationship and save our family.

And then they had to sit on the couch opposite their parents and be told that Mom and Dad weren't going to be married anymore. They had to watch Dad move out. They had to start sharing time, and they had to adjust to having two places to live. Then they had to move across the country, leaving their childhood home and all their friends behind. My past helped set in motion a chain of events that made life harder than it had to be for these two precious little men.

Fortunately, I was able to revive that part of me that was a good father. Less yelling, more loving, more focused. The boys began getting a better version of me during our reduced time together. I wasn't getting everything right, but I was pouring into them in a way that I had earlier in their lives. I was enjoying them, teaching them valuable life lessons, and feeling more connected.

That doesn't mean it was easy. The pressure inside to be as close to perfect as I could be for them was severe. In some ways, I felt like I had to make up for all the hurt and confusion they were subjected to because of the sudden revolving door of a life they had inherited. I found it difficult to balance loving them and leading them, between being their father and their friend. It is a tightrope on which all parents must balance, but in my situation, it was set much higher off the ground, stretched across shark-infested waters with high winds swaying it from side to side and driving rain blowing in sideways. That's how it felt anyway, like the margin of error was much less, and success was much harder to achieve. One misstep and more harm would be done.

My kiddos will pick this book up one day and hear the full story directly from me. They will get to see Dad in his weakness, in his humanity, in his brokenness. I don't know how they will respond, but I hope they see that while I veered off course and found myself on a desolate height, I had the courage to work my way back down the mountain. I hope I am able to model what it looks like to accept consequences, learn from mistakes, heal wounds, and do better the next time you have the chance. I hope they see that being a man isn't always about being strong and being right. It's about being you, telling the truth, standing for what you think is right, even if others think you're wrong, and admitting you're wrong when inevitably you are.

I hope I teach them to love people and always respond with grace. I hope they develop the ability to allow themselves to be human and offer another human being the opportunity to be human as well. I hope I can impart wisdom to them and ensure they understand the power of their specific stories, how to accept who they are, where they've been, what they've done, and how to engage with their calling. I hope they learn how to live authentically, how to be transparent, how to be rigorously honest with themselves and those who are in a relationship with them. I hope I can model the right way to recover from regrets, how to accept responsibility and cast aside shame, how to make amends and embark on new beginnings.

I hope they recall the wisest words I've ever said to them. This wisdom came directly from the pages of a children's book called *Put Me in the Zoo*. My older son would routinely fall asleep to this story when he was a toddler. Only when reflecting on my journey did I realize how prophetic and powerful that book is. It's about a rainbow-spotted leopard who more than anything wants to be placed in the zoo. That's where he will find his home, his comfort, his purpose. He's convinced the zoo will make him happy, and he's obsessed with finding a way to get there. At the end of the book, the main character finds his home. But it's the circus, not the zoo. He realizes the circus is where he was meant to be all along.

My kids watched their dad desperately trying to claw his way into the zoo when they were small. By the time they were entering double digits, they saw their dad finally realizing there was a circus waiting for him, and it was better than any zoo. My one goal in parenting these young men is to make sure they never settle for the comforts of this world at the expense of receiving the eternal calling that has been placed on their lives. The zoo is great. But it's no circus.

CHAPTER 27

Google Me

He stepped inside, eased the door shut, and looked out at me just above the rim of his glasses. Tell me about this "situation" you experienced last year.

A few weeks later, she sat across from me on the couch, face twisted with tears forming as she asked about "the article."

A few days after that, I sat with a third person. His eyes shifted left, then up toward the ceiling to avoid direct contact. His posture changed and was in complete misalignment with his words as he recited a string of clichés in response to my confession. Everyone makes mistakes. We're all human. It's how you respond and what you learn that matters. You just have to take it one day at a time. A cold, listless delivery not intended to comfort as much as to complete a checklist of what you need to say when someone tells you something you didn't want to hear.

These were the people in my life who were loving enough to offer me the chance to respond to my past. Two of them continued as an active part of my life. One professionally. The other personally. The third promised to be out there praying for me.

Within 48 hours of my arrest, more than 300 people had Googled my name to find the news article and see it for themselves. For those of you still mystified by the Internet and how it works, I will only say that once Google realizes that a certain link is popular for a certain search term, and that certain link is from a reputable source (i.e., a newspaper), its algorithm escorts such a link to the top of the pile, so as other people search for the same term, they are offered the most relevant and popular content associated with the term. Long story short, everyone I knew searched my name and read the article, making it the very first link anytime someone Googled my name.

For the next two years, every time I talked to someone in my extended network, made a new friend, connected with a new potential client or employer, or was interested in anyone romantically, I had to wonder. Have they seen it? When will they find it? When do I bring it up? Job interviews. New business proposals. A first date. Google became a relational land mine, ready to explode in my face at a moment's notice. It was a lose-lose proposition. If I introduced the topic into conversation too quickly, I risked not getting the chance to tell my story and appeal to the other person's understanding. If I waited too long, it appeared as if I were trying to hide it. For most people, it was so uncomfortable that they would conjure up excuses to cut conversations short or close out opportunities, all to avoid having to ask about what they found online. I missed out on a couple of shots at brokering an acquisition of my marketing agency because of the search results. Who knows how many jobs or clients steered clear once they found the news. More than a few, I'm estimating.

Even when someone afforded me the opportunity to address the arrest and share my story, it didn't fully alleviate the awkwardness of daily life. I routinely would find myself in social situations where I had no idea how many people around me knew about my past and less of an idea of what they thought about it. Everyone pretended to be unaware. I knew that wasn't true. So it was even more uncomfortable.

In my recovery, I had to come to grips with the shame that saddled me for most of my life. But always being followed by the Google search results left me feeling less than human. Inside, I knew most people had things they deeply regretted, secrets they would be horrified to have visible through a simple Web search. But their secrets were theirs to share or keep. I forfeited the luxury of making such decisions the moment I knocked on the door of Room 302. I know the full extent of what it's like to be Hester Prynne in *The Scarlet Letter*, wearing a glaring symbol to let everyone know that you have much to be ashamed of in your past, that you have failed, that you are flawed. It's like playing poker, but you are the only one showing your cards. Everyone else gets to keep their hands concealed while determining whether you are holding anything of value.

I am a marketing guy. That's how I've made a living for almost 20 years. I know a thing or two about the Internet, about how the news media work, about lots of things like that. If ever there was someone who could find a way to get an article removed from a Web search, or at least buried several pages deep, it's me. I tried it all. I came up empty. The article remained deeply entrenched in my online reputation. It outranked articles I had written for Fast Company, the homepage for my marketing firm, and dozens of other news media items that cast me in a positive light. Anything I tried to lessen its visibility amounted to throwing snowballs at an avalanche. Futile. Even as I was finalizing the first draft of this book, I took one last shot at it. Ran my request all the way up the flagpole of the parent company for the *Tennessean*. I was told it would be incongruent with the organization's journalistic integrity to remove a truthful report and that the public had a "right to know."

I fully completed the terms of my probation and had the arrest expunged. As far as the legal system is concerned, I have a clean record. The Internet begs to differ. My clean record is irrelevant in the face of my Google results, and it appears there is nothing I can do about it.

Part of me always knew this was also part of God's design. You see, if I had the option of disappearing into a happy, well-adjusted life where I could just be healthy and content and enjoy my family and friends and put all of this behind me, that's exactly what I would have done. I would have had grand plans to honor what I thought God was calling me to do. But I likely would never have finished this book. I would have grown complacent and comfortable and thankful to be free of this burden. The flames of my good intentions would have slowly transitioned into the slightest flicker and then eventually simmered into nothing but ashes.

But with the daily reminder from Google that this indeed is a story I would be required to tell, I was left with no choice other than share it as broadly as possible. At least then it would fulfill a purpose bigger than myself. If you are reading this, I believe the following statement is absolutely true. God intended for me to share this book with you for a very specific reason, to speak directly to you so that you (or someone you love) can reclaim your life.

The cost of that is chronic discomfort and the self-inflicted pressure of feeling like I have to defend every action and decision I make because everyone is already prepared to judge me. And trust me, people judge. I'm a Christian. I was a Bible-toting, church-attending, God-loving Christian all along the way. And that made it all the more atrocious to a lot of people.

Many times, the judgment is at a subconscious level, embedded just like all learned biases toward people who are different from you. There is a stigma attached to individuals who have a known struggle with addiction in any form. The first is this: Addicts are perceived as being exceptions. As noted earlier, pretty much everyone has an addiction of some shape, size, and intensity to deal with, or is in a relationship with someone who does. It's interesting how we've shaped a society that brands addicts as outcasts when their struggles originate from the very core of the human condition. The same defects are embedded in all of us. They are just waiting to be activated by a combination of external forces and internal turmoil. The vast majority of people in the throes of a significant battle with addiction aren't there simply because of bad choices. Yes, they failed to respond appropriately to circumstances in their lives, but many endured tragic experiences or lacked the basic knowledge and tools to respond in healthy ways. No one wakes up and determines they want to have an addiction problem anymore than anyone wakes up and expresses a desire to be homeless. It happens. Many times it happens so methodically that it isn't obvious that you need help until you need lots of help. And there is a lingering perception that addicts are broken down, worthless people who can't contribute to society. Truth be told, in recovery, I've become a better worker, father, friend, partner, and person than I ever was before. Living in truth, striving to improve my defects. Compassionate. In touch with my emotions. Present, most days. Yet, there is always a stigma.

That goes back to something I understand well as a marketing professional. The power of branding. Once you have a specific idea or belief about a company or a product, it takes a great deal to pry that from your mind. Conversely, once that idea or belief about a company or brand has been dislodged because of a scandal, a crisis, or a personal experience, you hardly ever return to the way you used to feel about it.

Addicts get hit from both sides. People who don't know you at all have tons of preconceived ideas and beliefs about "people like you." The people who know you well, who trusted you, will have a really hard time accepting that you are capable of change. That is the most challenging part about recovery. Only a select few will believe in your journey or see your progress or accept that there is more to you than what you've done. That's okay.

You ultimately only need one person to know you are healing. Only one person to believe you are doing all you can to be better.

Only one person to know that addiction no longer defines you and that you are working your way back down that desolate height. That person is *you*. Once you believe in yourself, God will lead people into your life who will care well for you, appreciate where you've been, and receive what you have to give. I've seen it happen. I know it's true.

In my situation, I've had to constantly remind myself that I am not alone. I keep in the front of my mind the fact that so many other people have taken similar, or worse, paths in response to similar, or worse, experiences from their pasts. My story just happens to be publicly available. I've had to remind myself that my sin does not define me, that we all get a chance to start over. I've had to remind myself that people's judgments of me have just as much to say about the state of their own hearts as they do about mine. I've had to remind myself that it is easy to assume people are judging me when maybe they aren't. I center on the fact that God has a specific purpose for me, to use my story to reach others. I have an opportunity to model vulnerability both to strangers as well as the people closest to me, starting with my two boys. These are the truths I've had to clothe myself with daily, until they felt like my own skin.

CHAPTER 28

Fear

I could feel my face warming, my blood pressure rising, my skin perspiring from every pore. The room was packed with small circles of people, chit-chatting as they sipped wine and cocktails and waited for the formal program to begin. I cut my eyes across the crowd and watched him weave his way along, shaking hands and patting backs and smiling widely. The rest of my circle carried on the conversation without me as I tracked his movement. Internally, I was pleading for him to go the opposite direction to the other end of the building. I was praying he wouldn't recognize me and that if he did, he'd be just as worried that I would recognize him.

As if he could sense my presence, he flipped a glance over his left shoulder and momentarily made eye contact with me. He cocked a slight grin with the side of his mouth, panned his eyes back across the room, and continued networking. I had a sudden surge of relief. And I needed to regroup. I excused myself from my wife and friends and retreated to the restroom. Alone, a wall of stalls behind me, urinals to my side and a row of sinks in front, I cupped hands full of water and splashed my face repeatedly. On the third scoop, the door flung open, and in he sauntered. Stopping two sinks down from me, he looked into the mirror and adjusted his sweater.

"Nice seeing you tonight, Heath."

He used my real name. Not the name he would know me by—the one I had used online. I paused, panicking on the inside. Who told him my name? Who do we both know? What would he do with this information? What did he want? My heart was throbbing, the water in my hands vibrating with every beat. I didn't say anything. I just nodded and stared straight ahead.

"Have fun tonight," he said as he gave his hair one last adjustment. "You look well." With those words, he exited the restroom.

Placing all my weight on the white sink, I pressed my hands until they were hot pink at the knuckles. I lowered my head, staring into the drain and wishing I could physically spiral inside and down it, swirling through the pipes to a completely different place. My eyes were ping-ponging beneath the lids as if I was swept up in a vivid dream. If only this was a dream. Then I could wake up. Then it could be over. As if it never happened.

There were approximately 450 random people assembled for the charity event that night. Friends of friends of friends. What were the chances that this man would be there? We had met a few weeks earlier at his office, after hours, for a brief and awkward encounter following a response to an online posting on Craigslist. I left that day, intending never to cross paths with him again, never even considering that I might not have a say in the matter. It was the first time my two worlds collided. And it was the most uncomfortable, anxiety-ridden, guilt-filled experience imaginable. For the rest of the night, he kept his distance, while I sat crippled with fear, circulating toxic levels of shame through my veins and obsessive thoughts through my brain.

Two days later

He was a beast of a man, with a round, bald, head and a scruffy beard. Dark, black sunglasses covered his eyes. He took up most of the cab of the large, white work truck he was driving. It was industrial strength with long toolboxes hanging off each side and thick steel bumpers. He was behind us for the better part of the ride home, but I didn't think much about it. There weren't a lot of paths to take. We were on the only main road. But after making two turns, he was still there. My heart sank. I was getting a bit suspicious. Just before the final turn that led to our neighborhood, I opted not to use my blinker and then made a sharp, last-minute turn. The hulking man in the white truck blew right by the street but then slammed on the brakes and threw it into reverse. This left me without any doubt. He was following us, and he wasn't happy.

I punched the gas. My family was in this vehicle, and I had no reason to believe this man just wanted to talk. We were going at least 60 miles per hour on a 20-miles-per-hour street, which was lined with houses. My wife was frozen, her eyes wide, her hands hanging on to the dash and the door. On the one hand, she really wanted to assume her usual duties as backseat driver. But on the other hand, she realized I was doing the only thing I could do—trying to get as far away from this man as I could. My sons (ages 8 and 5 at the time) seemed mostly oblivious in the back seat, just thinking that Dad was driving in sports mode again. It was all fun and games.

As my rearview mirror rattled, I trained an eye on it, watching nervously as the white truck kept pace, possibly getting closer. I shifted directions, ducking between rows of suburbia, left then right, right then left. When my rearview mirror finally failed to display our pursuant, I took two final turns and worked my way back to our house. We flew into the garage and closed the door.

Less than a minute later, the doorbell rang. My heart was in my throat this time. I drew a deep breath, keeping in my periphery an aluminum baseball bat that was propped against the front wall behind the front door. It was close enough if I needed it. I swallowed hard. I answered the door. To my relief, I opened it to find an annoyed but harmless neighbor, and no sign of the hulking man. Mr. Neighbor Guy was lecturing me on speeding through the neighborhood. I apologized and tried to explain the situation. He was hardly satisfied, probably thinking I made it up. I didn't care. He was walking away, and the burly beast was still nowhere to be seen. My heart was still pounding, but it seemed like we were safe.

On our drive home, I had cut off the guy in the work truck. He responded by honking his horn at me and expressing his displeasure. I responded with a middle finger out the driver's side window, filled with rage and not afraid to express it, or more accurately, unable to repress it. Responding poorly to my emotions put my entire family in danger, but I had little choice in the matter. I was at odds with myself, my actions regularly contradicting my desires for my life. The shame was steep within me. The fear was piling up as well. And the combination had me constantly on edge, ready to lash out. What transpired at the charity event a few nights earlier had been enough to push me off an emotional cliff. And off I went.

In her book *Codependent No More*, Melody Beattie wrote, "Feelings are emotional energy; they are not personality traits."[1] But left unchecked, they force themselves to come alive. When you repress feelings, they force their way out of you anyway in the form of compulsive, addictive, self-destructive behaviors. You didn't allow them to be expressed, so they decided to express themselves. That's never good, specifically when we're talking about fear.

Fear can be a trap that leads straight to hell. In a way, it's a gateway drug. It will progressively sabotage your thoughts, your actions, your entire life. Fear can prevent us from taking a chance on happiness. It also causes us to march in the exact opposite direction of happiness. Fear has a really strong grip. And once it's dug its nails into you, it is a struggle to escape.

Fear for me was multifaceted. I always stressed about finances, always worried I would be abandoned, always convinced myself that my life was going to come crashing down on me. Closely guarding dark secrets didn't help my multitude of phobias. I lived on the edge of panic daily, afraid I would be exposed for the fraud I was, paranoid I would be discovered and lose it all.

Pastor and author Robert Morgan describes fear well:

> Fear is like a skeletal hand that reaches into our chests, squeezing our hearts. This bony hand has many sharp fingers—anxiety, worry, anger, depression, obsession, compulsion, discouragement, jealousy, foreboding, phobia, timidity, mistrust, and that nagging sense of unease.[2]

It's interesting how one emotion can lead to others or have completely different symptoms. For example, as Morgan noted, for some, fear can come out as anxiety. For others, it shows up as anger. It's an emotion gifted to us for specific, appropriate, important uses. It's an emotion people don't handle properly.

My unexpressed emotions required an outlet. I would hold them down as long as possible before exploding, usually over the most insignificant of things, like my keys. Oh, my temper tantrums over not being able to find my keys! I can't even. It's too embarrassing.

But something magical happened when I began the healing process. As soon as I started tapping into those unexpressed emotions, my anger and rage evaporated. It happened overnight, a quickly won battle in the long-term war I was waging. An unexplained capacity to be patient and not explode. That pent-up anger was released into the atmosphere. Once I broke the seal, my emotions were able to exit in an orderly fashion. Once I shoved all those secrets out of the shadows and into the sunlight, I cleared a pathway for truth and acceptance to enter. Yes, I still get frustrated like everyone else on earth. But I no longer have to list anger as a character defect. It just disappeared, never to return. Because I'm engaging with my emotions. Because I've dealt with my past. Because I'm not constantly acting out of fear, trying to hide myself from the world. I'm an open book.

Oh, and my keys? Well, something else magically happened. I started putting my keys in a place I could find them. No more daily drama. I just pick up my keys and walk out the door. It's a brave new world.

I've learned that my emotions are a dashboard that informs me when something needs attention—much like the car you drive. When the oil light comes on, it's time for oil. When the temperature gauge enters the red, there's an issue somewhere. Your mind and body operate much like that car engine. If something is wrong, particularly something important, you need to pay attention to it and deal with it. Otherwise, you will reach a point where the engine will simply stop working altogether and require a costly trip to a mechanic. The difference in my life now, the biggest one, is that when I feel a specific emotion swell up in a way that demands attention, instead of blindly following it in an immediate response or ignoring it at all costs, I pause and ask, *Why am I feeling this?* I engage with it, feel my way through it. I listen to what that emotion is trying to tell me. I can't always make it go away, and I don't always respond in the perfect way. But because I know my story, because I'm processing pain, because I'm paying attention to my emotional dashboard, I'm able to make sense of things that once perplexed me in the most confusing ways.

"It's a glorious day when morning comes,
without the feeling of alarm."
——"1940," The Submarines

CHAPTER 29

Change

Dragons, winged horses, and other mythical creatures. Majestic birds flying through imaginary skies. Incredibly detailed calligraphy. Elaborate artwork tacked in layers across the walls of this cozy workspace. It was one of a series of chutes set to one side of a hallway, each offering a hint of privacy without being closed off and entirely secluded. A driving beat bumped along in the background. A sporadic buzzing that reminded me of a bug zapper cut in and out of the music. There was something hypnotic and calming about the bumping and the buzzing. The sounds almost had a sterile quality to them. White noise. A few short steps outside, a river of chaos was flowing down Ventura Boulevard, as it did every afternoon. But all the clamor of the city couldn't penetrate the heavily stickered front door with its iron bars and blacked-out windows.

He sat in a rolling chair, swiveling back and forth deliberately as he sketched out the pattern I was describing. He was clean-cut, surprisingly so. If he had body art of his own, it was well concealed. As he worked, I nervously looked around at some of his other drawings and almost felt guilty for not challenging his artistic abilities. Mine was a simple and crude idea. It was definitely not going to be his most exciting job ever. Nothing he'd likely place in his portfolio or even pin up on his wall. Yet he was focused, treating my request as if it were a call for a replica of the Sistine Chapel.

He held up the sketch to get my approval. Yep, it looked great. I wanted to throw up. I hate needles. I find it hard to give blood, and I always look away during movies or television shows when there's a shot of a patient getting stuck. The mere thought of sitting still while someone dug multiple needles into my skin repeatedly was so far outside of my comfort zone I couldn't fathom how I would have the gumption to go through with it. Moments later, he was ready to get started. Before I could slide out the side door and make a run for it, he had shaved a section of my left arm and was applying the stencil. And then, the needles. It hurt just as much as I thought it might. It felt like someone was dragging a butter knife across my skin until they drew blood. Repeated movements, back and forth. After an eternity (which was probably 10 minutes tops), he paused, cracked his neck, and examined his efforts. Thank goodness that's over, I thought to myself. I looked over for the first time during the process. To my dismay, he had only outlined the letters. He still had to fill them in!

After he finished filling them in, I peeked over again and was very satisfied with what I saw. I let my eyes run over it several times. My first tattoo. Probably my last tattoo. But this one was important. I had contemplated getting it for at least a year. Finally, I had summoned the courage.

(t)here

Yep, that's all it says. It's very symbolic for me. If you want to get to "there," wherever that happens to be, you have to start "here." In its simplest form, it's a pneumonic device I've used to remind me to be present. To take the small steps today that will lead to big results in the future. To live the life in front of me and not spend too much time worrying about a future that hasn't even been promised. I meditate on this so often that I wanted to have a daily reminder tattooed on me so I would never forget. To get to there, I must start here.

That's how it works when you are trying to recover. When you are trying to transform your life. When you are trying to find your way down from a desolate height. When you are trying to truly live your days differently than you did before.

Which leads me to a philosophical question.

Can a person change?

In my attempt to evolve, I've had equal parts triumph and tragedy, blessing and curse, right and wrong, success and failure. But through it all, my answer to this question would be an emphatic *YES!*

But it's hard. Incredibly hard. And there are obstacles. And you don't eradicate those dark places within you, no matter how much you take away their power to influence your path forward. It's where the whole leopard-changing-its-spots saying comes from. You are who you are—an imperfect, broken, flawed individual—with unlimited potential to rise above and even leverage the things that make you imperfect.

But you will fail. Miserably. Often. Stumble around. Trip. You won't get it right most of the time. At least not at first. Some people will use your ongoing imperfection as evidence that you haven't changed at all. Partly because they have been burned by other people in their past and are skeptical. Partly because they don't really want to believe someone else can change if they can't (or won't). Partly because they don't want to let go of the past and relinquish their perceived power and control. You can't listen to those people in your life.

Yes, we can change. We all do. All the time. And it will take a while for your change to look like anything more than a messy, awkward, error-ridden, futile attempt. But it will take shape, if you persevere.

That truth was a hard-fought one for me in recovery. One of the potentially flawed aspects of the 12-step model is the ritualistic celebration of consecutive sobriety versus cumulative sobriety. In 12-step meetings, when a person has passed certain milestones of maintaining sobriety, they receive group praise and rewards in the form of "chips" that represent periods of time (i.e., one week, one month, two months, etc.).

Conversely, if you've "slipped" in your recovery in any way, you are expected to confess that to the group, or at the very least your sponsor and accountability partners. I understand the design here. Withdrawing from bad habits, establishing a new normal, establishing consistency—all of those things are necessary and require days of sobriety to be stacked one upon another. But for me, anything less than a perfect recovery walk (which isn't realistic or even possible) left me feeling like I was getting nowhere. The shame re-entered those well-worn paths inside of me and started marching up and down to wreak havoc as if it never had vacated my body. This was a point of tension for me until a therapist pointed out what I had accomplished in terms of cumulative sobriety. He pulled out a calendar and asked, "How many days were you sober this year? How many days were you present and actively working to better yourself? How many days were you aware of your emotions and able to respond differently to them than you did in the past?" My answer was 359. Out of 365 days, I had a small handful of mild infractions that would be considered a "slip" based on the behavior I was addressing. Then the icing on the cake. He asked, "How many days could you report being sober in the previous year?" Hmmm. I wasn't sure, but the answer had to be rapidly approaching *zero*.

It's not about getting everything perfect. It's about progress.

I have days when I feel like I'm running in mud. Others when I'm gliding on ice. But mostly, it's one foot in front of the other. I often have to fight the urge to defend myself in the face of those who doubt me. I often have to fight the urge to beat myself up when I don't respond to life's challenges perfectly. I often fight the paralyzing guilt and shame that comes with realizing I let everyone in my life down, including my family, my friends, my professional connections, and even myself. I often fight the urge to listen to those voices, the same ones that used to tell me I was unworthy. They evolved, as they always do. Finding new lies to tell. Now they say I can't do this. That no one believes I can do this. That I can't overcome this.

But I fight all those urges. And more times than not, I win. Because the simple truth is that behaviors and habits that once ruled my life with an iron fist have fully lost their ability to hold even the weakest of grips on the person I am today.

On October 9, 2015, I had a light-switch moment. Suddenly, there was brightness all around me, and I could clearly see for the first time, as if a light switch had been flipped up to wash away the darkness that had me confined and confused. I jumped at the chance to be free. God made it easy by stripping away all the idols in my life, all the places I historically turned to for comfort—my marriage, my professional reputation, my ability to perform and project. I no longer had the fear of losing what was valuable to me as an impediment, as a force keeping me trapped in my sickness. It was an easy choice. I saw it as a second chance. And I've tried to make the most of it. I dove in, made radical adjustments to my daily routine, pushed the healing process to its fastest possible speed and did everything asked of me in recovery. I went all in, all at once. I had been waiting for those chains to be undone, for that cage door to fly open. When it did, I ran. No looking back. Your change process might look just like mine, or it might look very different. But I know this. It will be one foot in front of the other. You won't do it perfectly. But you will change. Absolutely. You will. If you remember one simple truth. The way to there, starts here.

CHAPTER 30

Homeless

Lower Wacker Drive. Chicago. 10:00 p.m. on a Tuesday.

Wind was hurtling through like an invisible freight train, funneling between the walls of the underpass, a biting cold that ripped flesh from your face as it passed by you. Peering out from under the road, cars humming above, I could see a beautiful cityscape, heavenward structures, new construction, lights, and hustle and bustle. Decadence.

It's not unfathomable that someone could walk the distance of this street and never see another soul, even though they would have been surrounded on the entire journey. The homeless were huddled and hiding behind posts, in corners, beneath boxes and blankets. Anywhere that concealed their presence and blocked the wind.

But my companion this winter night knew the place well. He knew every person by name. He knew exactly where they would be, just as if they had a physical address on a suburban street. I was tagging along to help with his regular pilgrimage, handing out food, clothing, and supplies. Anything that might help our fellow brothers and sisters more readily handle another night.

We met all kinds of people. I wondered about many of their stories, how they ended up here, what their dreams were, what it would take for them to get back on their feet. Not all of them started on the streets. Not all of them came from a background that put them at risk, although many obviously fit that description. We passed a group of young men, and a few women. Late teens even. They had their own little community going. My guide explained that they were suburban youth who had become addicted to heroin. And now here they were.

I pictured them all cleaned up, in current fashions. Driving Range Rovers. Going to pool parties. Filling out college applications. Playing Xboxes. Yet here they were, riddled by the side effects of drug addiction, scraping along the underbelly of downtown just a few miles away from families who likely had no idea what had become of them. I felt compassion for every single person we encountered that night, many of whom wrestled with addiction or abuse or serious mental and medical conditions, or just a horrific string of bad luck. But none captured my attention more than these troubled teens. They reminded me of me. They had the trappings of what the world would have considered "a good life." But it didn't comfort them. They couldn't rest in it and be content. They were hurting or bored, and they had a hole inside that needed to be filled. I shivered. The hole had only grown wider and deeper and darker. It had swallowed them from the outside in.

Just as it once had swallowed me.

Later on, I stood beside a purring sedan, its exhaust puffing as the heater tried to keep up with the icy air entering through rolled down windows. In that moment, a little more than a year after my arrest, clarity swept over me and mixed into the freezing wind.

If you are still, if you are strong and steadfast, His calling will be as obvious as a beam of light in darkness—His pull as strong as the ocean's tide. You will be overwhelmed with an abundance of joy and the fulfillment of promises. But to start, you must stop. To play, you must pause. God will reveal His plans for you.

Be quiet.

That's what I did that night. I was quiet. And I received confirmation of the path God wanted me to take, the people God wanted me to help, and the purpose my pain could fulfill.

That night it was confirmed to me that I am to be a light. That I was expected to stand up and share my story. I was bought at a price, not to become a slave to worldly things but to be free.

> But you, brethren, are not in darkness, so that this Day should overtake you as a thief. You are all sons of light and sons of the day. We are not of the night nor of darkness. Therefore let us not sleep, as others *do*, but let us watch and be sober. For those who sleep, sleep at night, and those who get drunk are drunk at night. But let us who are of the day be sober, putting on the breastplate of faith and love, and as a helmet the hope of salvation.
>
> —1 Thess. 5:4–8

American author David Foster Wallace once wrote this about freedom and where you find it: "The really important kind of freedom involves attention, and awareness, and discipline, and effort, and being able truly to care about other people and to sacrifice for them, over and over, in myriad petty little unsexy ways, every day."[1]

Despite his wisdom and insights on life and meaning, Wallace succumbed to a decades-long fight with depression and committed suicide in September 2008. He was 46 years old. An accomplished writer. Well on his way to carving out a place for himself in literary history that few authors enjoy. He had a deep understanding of how we should approach healing and happiness. But he never got the hang of riding that backwards bicycle.

These are the stakes. We face those unmet needs, those unresolved traumas, those untapped emotions, or we die. Either a death executed by our own hands, an untimely end because of consequences we invited into our lives, or, more commonly, a slow ascent to a desolate height where we die simply from not ever really living. Where our consciousness slowly slips away and falls behind. Where the light gradually fades until we no longer see ourselves or others around us. Numb. Cold. Then dead.

I'm choosing to live, which means I have to heal. The best way I've found to do that is to help. To have a heart for others. To carry empathy into every conversation, interaction, transaction, and altercation. To encourage anyone I meet to chase down their devils, purge themselves of the small-g gods in their lives, and to embark on the slow, steady, soul-filling experience of climbing down to solid ground.

Yes, I'm working on my own junk while I practice this, but trust me when I say that every kind gesture, every loving approach, every thoughtful word brings me closer to experiencing the fullest, truest, best version of me. I am on this journey with you. I have a long way to go. But I'm leaning in, every day. And it's working.

I will leave you with this. In the dire poverty of the human condition, in all the misguided passions of the flesh, if you look closely and think clearly, you can't help but see the undeniable power and the unlimited potential of the spirit within you. The problem is that too many times, we focus on the emptiness and the futility of the former at the expense of receiving the fullness and abundance of the latter.

As it turns out, the darkness I was capable of in my depravity can't compete with or compare to the light that can shine in and through me. I can't tell you with any certainty where my story takes me next. What I can say is that I am free. I am a light. I will shine. I will find my dream. My prayer is that soon you can say the same.

Tools & Resources

My Unprofessional Opinion

I offer encouragement and examination of experiences in this book. What I don't do is provide professional-grade counseling or psychological intervention. Some who read this will be fortunate enough to be in an early stage of addiction, or just far enough from their path that they can still see the way back. For others, more substantial help might be needed.

If you find yourself with a dependency relationship you find impossible to break (whether that be alcohol, drugs, sex, gambling, etc.), please consider engaging with a trained professional who has direct experience helping individuals process out of addictive situations. There are many forms of counseling that can prove helpful, ranging from individual sessions to group therapy to intense inpatient experiences. I urge you to not rely solely on your willpower or the advice of friends and family or a 12-step program. Or even books like this one.

If you feel you are out of options, that life isn't worth the trouble, that there is no hope, let me say this. Please don't give up. Your life has value. Your life has meaning. You have a purpose, a specific purpose waiting to be unlocked. I don't dare presume to understand what it's like for you. What I do know is that I've met countless individuals who once felt the pain was far too great but now are experiencing joy beyond joy. I've had days where the thought crossed my mind that maybe everyone else would be better off without me in the picture. No matter how far you've gone, no matter what you've done or what's been done to you, giving up isn't the answer. Before you decide I'm wrong, talk to someone who can help.

Before I wrap things up here, I want to share a small gift. In the following pages, you'll find resources and tools that have been invaluable to me during my journey. It is by no means an exhaustive set of strategies. But if you apply these truths in your own journey, I think you'll find that climbing down from your desolate height will be a more agile and expedient process.

5 Lies You Are Telling Yourself Right Now

Lies are alive and well inside of you. There are specific lies you are telling yourself that were born and nurtured from your personal experiences and beliefs. And then, there are lies largely common for anyone who's struggling with emotional instability, addiction, or dependency relationships. Here are five big ones you need to face head on:

1. **I don't have a problem.** Yes, you do.
2. **It's not safe for me to get help.** Isolation is the name of the game. Your addiction will want you to feel there is no one and nowhere safe to turn to for help.
3. **I have too much to lose.** You are guaranteed to lose more and more of the things you care about the longer you wait to get help. It's like chasing a bad hand in poker. The money on the table is already gone. If you don't fold, you just keep giving more away.
4. **I can do it by myself.** No, you can't.
5. **I've done too much damage already.** Your behaviors will become progressive, more frequent, more intense. If you don't get help, you will endure a long, slow, painful ascent into self-destruction. If you do get help, you can experience healing and redemption in your life. Beauty from the ashes.

13 Truths to Recovery

I don't have all the answers, but I have learned a lot about the process of recovery. Here are some absolute truths that you will discover for yourself as you embark on this journey to reclaim your life.

1. **You must be broken.** Sitting at rock bottom. If you aren't in a desperate place, committed at all costs, this isn't going to work.

2. **Before you fight, you must surrender.** The longer you fight, the deeper the hooks go and the more pain. You aren't getting off the hook. The fish in the catch-and-release pond doesn't realize he is getting freedom—and wisdom—from the hook experience. He doesn't know he's getting cast back into the water, wounded but wise. He just knows he wants to return to his life and have a second chance. You are that fish, squirming for a second chance. You won't succeed until you surrender.

3. **You must be "all in."** As it says in 1 Corinthians 9:24, you have to run like you want to win the race. You have to fight like you can't afford to lose. Because you can't. If you approach recovery with the uncertainty of one who punches the air, you will be defeated. Isaiah 28:6 says that strength will be given to those who will chase the enemy not just out of their own city, but all the way back to the enemy's own gate. You have to commit fully to a new way of living. As they say in 12-step groups, half-measures will avail nothing. It will require all of you. All the time.

4. **You are not alone, and you can't do it alone.** You must battle the shame, the lies that say you are messed up and no one else is. You have to find others who have experienced similar things. Glean wisdom and encouragement and acceptance from them.

5. **You will need to perfect your patience.** Recovery won't move as fast as you want it to, and you can't do anything to make it go faster. But when you are in darkness, you have His promises. There is eternal life waiting for those who can practice "patient continuance" (Rom. 2:7).

6. **The path ahead goes through the past.** Remember, life is a labyrinth, not a maze. You've been walking in the wrong direction, ascending to a desolate height. The only way ahead is back. You have to return to the path God has for you. Back from whence you came, in other words. Retracing your steps, re-encountering the most painful parts of your past, will be key to your healing and instrumental in equipping you for a happy, joyful, productive existence.

7. **It won't be what you expected.** Plot twists, alternate endings, surprises. I entered recovery with far different expectations and desires than what God had for me in the end. You will see this, too. Even when we think big, we think small. Be open to the idea that God dreams bigger than you do and that your plans are not necessarily His.

8. **Sometimes you will slip, and that's okay.** I believe in cumulative sobriety versus consecutive. That means not focusing on the isolated incidents when you make a bad choice in your recovery, but instead focusing on the transformation that is taking place. When climbing down from a desolate height to reclaim your life, you will slip from time to time. It is a steep incline with treacherous footing. But if handled properly, even a slip can bring you closer to the ground. You will learn that it can be progress even when it isn't perfection. You slip, and then you get your footing again and continue.

9. **Clarity will come in pieces.** The closer you get to the ground and the more engaged you are with your story, the more visibility you will have for your life moving forward. Even

so, understand that God's plan for your life is so big that there's no way to take it all in. Faith is the belief of things yet to be seen (Heb. 11:1). Your life's purpose will unfold in front of you, one step at a time. Piece by piece. That is by design. Faith is required.

10. **It is going to hurt.** A lot. But there's a point to the pain. Affliction comes from the consequence of sin (we talked about the long tail of sin earlier). It also comes in the form of opposition as you pursue God's will. Just because you decide to start with a clean slate doesn't mean it won't be complicated. Opportunity will not be without obstacles. An awakening will still see adversity—require it, even. This is going to be a violent process. A battle. Resistance. Warfare. You are removing a cancer from your body. You are purifying your soul. You are swimming against the current. You are under attack. You are receiving correction from God. As described in Micah 1:3–4, God is treading on your high places, destroying them so utterly that he wrecks their foundation, sapping the power of idols, shining light on secrets, leveling mountains. But it is in faithfulness that you have been afflicted (Ps. 119:75). It's for your greater good. There will be payment that outreaches and overcompensates for all the pain you endure, all the affliction that comes your way. It all will have a purpose to craft you into the being you were meant to be and lead you to the promises God has for you.

11. **You aren't wrestling against flesh and blood** (Eph. 6:12). The enemy is not of this world. You must battle seduction, misdirection, brainwashing, distraction, fearmongering, mind alteration, falsehoods, propaganda, and shaming in order to avoid being snared in addiction and taken out of your own life. Luckily, the weapons at your disposal are not of this world either (2 Cor. 10:3–4).

12. **Don't mistake a milestone for your ultimate mission.** Stopping the bad habits and unacceptable behaviors is just the start. You have to fill the hole inside of you. You have to pull the problem up from the roots. Your addiction was just a symptom that something else was wrong. So don't settle on sobriety as the ultimate measure of your success. It's merely a foundational step to where you want to go. Celebrate milestones, but never lose sight of your mission. Keep pressing forward.

13. **You are guaranteed success.** How about that! Nowhere else in life will you receive such a sure thing. If you surrender, if you seek, if you step, you will see His promises fulfilled. In his book *Redemption*, Mike Wilkerson puts it nicely. "Your redemption is as certain as his resurrection."[1] God will not rest until his promise is fulfilled (Isa. 62:1–4).

Holistic Healing – The Day Ahead

You live your life like you live your days. Want to change your life? Change today! Here's a list ripped from my calendar to get you started. Don't let the size of this list suggest that it will take you all day. Much of this is habit-based and can be easily integrated into your life. However, don't try to implement all of these all at once. Build your way toward a day packed with health and healing.

1. **Nutrition** – Clean up your diet. Less processed foods. More clean options. Real food (fruits, vegetables, etc.).

2. **Fitness** – Commit to regular exercise, whether a 30-minute workout at home, long walks or runs, trips to the gym. Make sure movement is part of your schedule.

3. **Quiet Time, Meditation** – Carve out a specific time of day, preferably first thing in the morning, and practice being still and hearing from God. You can read scripture, journal, meditate, or pray. Just quiet your mind and let go. This is a great time for resetting your mind and body, for self-reflection, and for strengthening your faith.

4. **Reading** – Continue to increase your understanding of addiction, spirituality, emotional intelligence, and other related topics by always having a book you're working through for the specific purpose of improving yourself in some way.

5. **Sponsor/Step Work** – Follow a 12-step program. It doesn't matter which one. Just choose a flavor of this process that fits you and stick with it. While not a perfect model, step work will push you to answer critical questions about yourself and provide a road map for you to achieve a higher state of being.

6. **Community** – Find a small circle of people who can offer you unconditional support, either through an existing set of friends, your local church, or a 12-step program. Find ways

to get more involved in your community as well, and limit the opportunity you have to isolate yourself.

7. **Vision Board** – Create a vision board of what you want to accomplish in your life in the year ahead, and revisit it every single day. Make sure you include professional pursuits and personal goals.

8. **Bottom-Line Behaviors** – Compile a list of specific behaviors, actions, or attitudes you want to fully eradicate from your life. These items become your bottom-line behaviors, which means you will avoid them at all costs and talk to someone if you slip up.

9. **Love Yourself** – Be kind to yourself. It sounds cheesy, but you need to show yourself a little love. Personal affirmations are a great way to go. Keep them in your wallet, or on a wall, or on your car dashboard.

10. **Love Others** – Whenever you have a chance, be kind to others. Be a light. Be a smile in a crowd of frowns. Model the way you'd like to be treated. Give. Then, you get. Seek out opportunities to compliment someone, to forgive someone, to help someone, to let someone know they aren't alone.

11. **Practice Gratitude** – Instead of focusing on what's wrong or not right, be grateful. Thank God for what He's provided. Be appreciative of the big and small things you have. Be content where you are. Rest in who you are today.

12. **Establish Rituals and Memorials** – Set up rituals where you attach significance and meaning to specific activities. For me, it was making the bed. This was something I never did before recovery, but every morning since starting my journey, I wake up and make the bed. It is a subtle action that puts me right back into stepping forward with my plan. You can also create memorials where you assign meaning to a photo or painting or other possession to serve as a

continual reminder. Some people put pictures of their kids on the dashboard of their cars. Others carry a card or coin in their wallet. I affixed a daily affirmation statement to my bathroom mirror so I would receive words every day that triggered my consciousness.

Storyboard

Creating an inventory of the negatives in your life can be the best positive step toward a better version of you. The worksheet on the following page can prove extremely helpful in mapping your past to understand your present and improve your future. First, let's define each of the terms you need to examine:

Unmet Needs – Basic desires embedded in humanity, such as affirmation, safety, acceptance. What needs have gone unmet in your life?

Unresolved Trauma – Instances of abuse or betrayal. These can be significant or subtle—anything that was traumatic enough to have a lingering, adverse effect.

Untapped Emotions – Shame, fear, what are the emotions you can't seem to control? What parts of your emotional dashboard are lighting up and running hot on a regular basis?

Negative Self-Beliefs – What are the lies you tell yourself? Some common examples are "I'm not worthy," "I'm not lovable," "I will be abandoned."

Character Defects – What are the parts of yourself that need self-reflection and improvement? Envy, jealously, selfishness? You likely have a long list of defects, but what are the ones causing the most strife in your life and your relationships?

Triggers – What are the sights, smells, memories, thoughts, situations that prompt pain for you, that create the need for you to escape or retreat? What matches light the fuse of your sufferings?

Coping Mechanisms – What do you do when faced with pain? Do you isolate? Do you shut down? Do you rage? How do you cope?

Idols – Who or what in your life do you lean on and expect to save you? A spouse? Work? Possessions? What are you relying on as a substitute for God?

Addictions – What vices have emerged in your life as you've tried to cope with your past and your pain? Alcohol? Drugs? Sex? Gambling? Social media? Food?

Storyboard Inventory Worksheet

Unmet Needs	Unresolved Trauma	Untapped Emotions
Negative Self-Beliefs	Character Defects	Triggers
Coping Mechanisms	Idols	Addictions

Ascending to Addiction

The following model for addiction and the accompanying illustration were created out of the collective insights of my own experiences, as well as wisdom from counselors, support groups, and the research and writings of leaders in the addiction and recovery space. Specifically, I found reflections of my experiences, my emotions, and my expedition to a desolate height within the writings of Patrick Carnes[2] and Mark Laaser.[3]

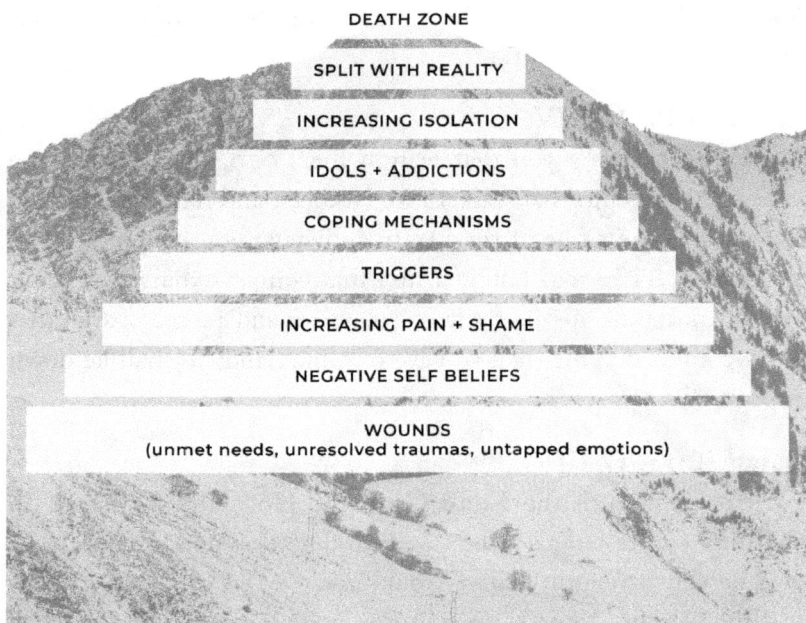

DEATH ZONE

SPLIT WITH REALITY

INCREASING ISOLATION

IDOLS + ADDICTIONS

COPING MECHANISMS

TRIGGERS

INCREASING PAIN + SHAME

NEGATIVE SELF BELIEFS

WOUNDS
(unmet needs, unresolved traumas, untapped emotions)

Scripture

Many passages of scripture have spoken deeply to me during my descent from my desolate height. Here are my favorites. I have listed them without commentary as I believe in the living aspect of the word. I have no doubt they will speak to you in powerful yet different ways than they did to me. I recommend taking one verse at a time and meditating on it for a week in order to receive the biggest impact.

John 16:33 KJV

"These things I have spoken unto you, that in me ye might have peace. In the world ye shall have tribulation: but be of good cheer; I have overcome the world."

Isaiah 50:10–11 KJV

"Who is among you that feareth the Lord, that obeyeth the voice of his servant, that walketh in darkness, and hath no light? let him trust in the name of the Lord, and stay upon his God.

Behold, all ye that kindle a fire, that compass yourselves about with sparks: walk in the light of your fire, and in the sparks that ye have kindled. This shall ye have of mine hand; ye shall lie down in sorrow."

Isaiah 30:15–17 KJV

"For thus saith the Lord God, the Holy One of Israel; In returning and rest shall ye be saved; in quietness and in confidence shall be your strength: and ye would not.

But ye said, No; for we will flee upon horses; therefore shall ye flee: and, We will ride upon the swift; therefore shall they that pursue you be swift.

One thousand shall flee at the rebuke of one; at the rebuke of five shall ye flee: till ye be left as a beacon upon the top of a mountain, and as an ensign on a hill."

Ecclesiastes 3:11 KJV

"He hath made everything beautiful in his time: also he hath set the world in their heart, so that no man can find out the work that God maketh from the beginning to the end."

Ecclesiastes 7:13 KJV

"Consider the work of God: for who can make that straight, which he hath made crooked?"

1 Corinthians 1:25 KJV

"Because the foolishness of God is wiser than men; and the weakness of God is stronger than men."

1 Corinthians 9:24 KJV

"Know ye not that they which run in a race run all, but one receiveth the prize? So run, that ye may obtain."

Job 5:17 KJV

"Behold, happy is the man whom God correcteth: therefore despise not thou the chastening of the Almighty."

Job 26:7 KJV

"He stretcheth out the north over the empty place, and hangeth the earth upon nothing."

Hebrews 11:1 KJV

"Now faith is the substance of things hoped for, the evidence of things not seen."

2 Corinthians 12:9 KJV

"And he said unto me, My grace is sufficient for thee: for my strength is made perfect in weakness. Most gladly therefore will I rather glory in my infirmities, that the power of Christ may rest upon me."

2 Corinthians 8:10 KJV

"And herein I give my advice: for this is expedient for you, who have begun before, not only to do, but also to be forward a year ago."

Luke 12:48 KJV

"But he that knew not, and did commit things worthy of stripes, shall be beaten with few stripes. For unto whomsoever much is given, of him shall be much required: and to whom men have committed much, of him they will ask the more."

Matthew 10:27 KJV

"What I tell you in darkness, that speak ye in light: and what ye hear in the ear, that preach ye upon the housetops."

1 Corinthians 14:33 KJV

"For God is not the author of confusion, but of peace, as in all churches of the saints."

Romans 5:1–5 KJV

"Therefore being justified by faith, we have peace with God through our Lord Jesus Christ: By whom also we have access by faith into this grace wherein we stand, and rejoice in hope of the glory of God. And not only so, but we glory in tribulations also: knowing that tribulation worketh patience; And patience, experience; and experience, hope: And hope maketh not ashamed; because the love of God is shed abroad in our hearts by the Holy Ghost which is given unto us."

2 Corinthians 1:8–10 KJV

"For we would not, brethren, have you ignorant of our trouble which came to us in Asia, that we were pressed out of measure, above strength, insomuch that we despaired even of life: But we had the sentence of death in ourselves, that we should not trust in ourselves, but in God which raiseth the dead: Who delivered us from so great a death, and doth deliver: in whom we trust that he will yet deliver us."

Jeremiah 33:3 KJV

"Call unto me, and I will answer thee, and show thee great and mighty things, which thou knowest not."

Psalm 16:11 KJV

"Thou wilt shew me the path of life: in thy presence *is* fulness of joy; at thy right hand there are pleasures for evermore."

Hebrews 13:5 KJV

"Let your conversation be without covetousness; and be content with such things as ye have: for he hath said, I will never leave thee, nor forsake thee."

Hebrews 10:31–39 KJV

"It is a fearful thing to fall into the hands of the living God.

But call to remembrance the former days, in which, after ye were illuminated, ye endured a great fight of afflictions; Partly, whilst ye were made a gazingstock both by reproaches and afflictions; and partly, whilst ye became companions of them that were so used. For ye had compassion of me in my bonds, and took joyfully the spoiling of your goods, knowing in yourselves that ye have in heaven a better and an enduring substance. Cast not away therefore your confidence, which hath great recompence of reward. For ye have need of patience, that, after ye have done the will of God, ye might receive the promise.

For yet a little while, and he that shall come will come, and will not tarry.

Now the just shall live by faith: but if any man draw back, my soul shall have no pleasure in him.

But we are not of them who draw back unto perdition; but of them that believe to the saving of the soul."

Galatians 5:1 KJV

"Stand fast therefore in the liberty wherewith Christ hath made us free, and be not entangled again with the yoke of bondage."

2 Corinthians 5:17 KJV

"Therefore if any man be in Christ, he is a new creature: old things are passed away; behold, all things are become new."

2 Corinthians 4:16 KJV

"For which cause we faint not; but though our outward man perish, yet the inward man is renewed day by day."

Joshua 1:3 KJV

"Every place that the sole of your foot shall tread upon, that have I given unto you, as I said unto Moses"

Ephesians 4:31–32 KJV

"Let all bitterness, and wrath, and anger, and clamour, and evil speaking, be put away from you, with all malice: And be ye kind one to another, tenderhearted, forgiving one another, even as God for Christ's sake hath forgiven you."

Matthew 10:39 KJV

"He that findeth his life shall lose it: and he that loseth his life for my sake shall find it."

Matthew 4:16 KJV

"The people which sat in darkness saw great light; and to them which sat in the region and shadow of death light is sprung up."

Romans 8:28 KJV

"And we know that all things work together for good to them that love God, to them who are the called according to his purpose."

Philippians 1:6 KJV

"Being confident of this very thing, that he which hath begun a good work in you will perform it until the day of Jesus Christ."

Reading List

There are so many great books out there to help you heal. I've mentioned several within this book, but here's my reading list from the past five years. These authors have had a tremendous influence on my life.

Wide Awake by Erwin Raphael McManus

Redemption by Mike Wilkerson

On the Threshold of Transformation by Richard Rohr

The Naked Now by Richard Rohr

To Be Told by Dan B. Allender

The Wounded Healer by Henri J.M. Nouwen

Wild at Heart by John Eldredge

Healing the Shame That Binds Us by John Bradshaw

Healing the Wounds of Sexual Addiction by Mark Laaser

Out of the Shadows by Patrick J. Carnes

The Big Book by Alcoholics Anonymous

The Book of Isaiah

Quick-Start Curriculum for Your Daily Quiet Time

I suggest you start each day with 15 minutes of meditation and 15 minutes reading scripture. Feel free to go above and beyond, but this will be a great starting point for those of you starting from scratch in a daily spiritual walk. Even those of you who have more experience engaging with God will find value here. So often we need to go back to the foundation and relearn the basics.

The following three-week calendar focuses on establishing faith, finding peace, and experiencing joy. This spiritual trifecta is a great foundation for living life to the fullest. These three elements work together. You can't have one without the others. Also, each of these elements strengthens the others, so as you grow in one, the natural response is growth and strength in the other two.

WEEK 1, DAY 1 – Hebrews 11:1

This verse says faith is the substance of things hoped for and evidence of things not seen. Meditate on this verse today and ask yourself some basic questions about your belief systems.

- What do you really believe to be true about God?
- What do you have faith in when it comes to God?
- Why do you believe what you believe?

It's important to get a quick temperature check and assess where you are in your belief system before you push ahead. What's your starting point in this journey? That will determine the order of your steps.

WEEK 1, DAY 2 – Isaiah 28:10

Your spiritual journey is a lot like grass growing. It's going to be a slow, methodical march. You won't necessarily see it daily, but over time, you'll experience a lush field of green. This is transformative change, but it is not a light switch that goes from off to on.

You have to build. This passage points to precept upon precept, little by little, and that is exactly what you are doing here. One step, one building block at a time.

Reflect today on your answers to yesterday's belief questions. Revisit why you started this journey. Spend a few moments in silence and see what God has for you today.

WEEK 1, DAY 3 – Mark 9:24, James 1:23

Of course, none of us has perfect faith. But that's okay. This is one of my favorite passages on faith. "I believe; help my unbelief!"

Want more faith?

There are two easy things you can do. The first is to take action.

Faith without works is dead. James says you are blessed when you do, so don't just sit there waiting for faith. Do something. Take action. Work. Move. Lean forward. Push. God will show up.

And then—ask God! We can have honest conversations with Him. When we are lacking in faith or feel like we aren't trusting enough in Him, we need to speak that and ask for help.

What is one area of your life that creates fear in you? One problem you aren't relying on God to handle? One sin you just can't shake?

Today, take one thing directly to God and ask for more faith in His ability to help you with it. Ask specifically for more faith. Don't ask for Him to fix it or take it away. Ask Him to give you confidence that He can handle it and that He will handle it, in His time and in His way.

Meditate after you've made this request. Wait and hear from God.

WEEK 1, DAY 4 – Mark 11:23

Jesus says that whoever says to this mountain "be removed and be cast into the sea" and does not doubt in his heart will see it happen.

God is not interested in doing small things in your life. His promises are grand. He wants to move mountains and cast them into the sea. Think big. What are the mountains in your life? The biggest, toughest, more challenging climbs that lie ahead? The most painful parts of your past? When you stand firm, without doubt, God will move those mountains for you.

The passage goes on to say that what you ask for when you pray, you will receive. So in prayer, we find our faith. We reduce our doubts. We build strength. Spend some concentrated time today praying for God to remove your doubt. Speak out about the mountains you need cast into the sea. Ask Him what promises He wants to make to you and what vision He has for your future. He will show you!

WEEK 1, DAY 5 – 1 Corinthians 14:33

The truth for today is simple. God is not an author of confusion. He speaks clearly. There is a lot of noise in our world, and even more noise between our ears. There are competing messages, lies, distractions, distortions, differing opinions, contradictory truths. The chaos of our daily lives, coupled with the turmoil of our inner self, creates a situation where it's almost impossible to hear from God. That doesn't change the fact that He is speaking. Softly. Confidently. Clearly.

That's why it is so important to spend time every single day in a quiet place with God. Listening for his instruction. If we can quiet our minds, we will hear Him. And we will know we are hearing from Him because there will be no confusion or nonsense in the message. No riddle for us to unwind. No clutter to add to the pile. It will be clear, discernible truth. If you are hearing something else, stop listening. That's not God!

WEEK 1, DAY 6 – Job 11:7, Proverbs 3:5–6

Remember, faith is evidence of things unseen. God is far too vast and powerful to fully grasp. When we try to put God in a box and rationalize our beliefs, we are in big trouble. That's not faith. Instead, "lean not on your own understanding" but allow God to direct your path. You don't have to have it figured out. It doesn't have to make sense. You can't be sure and certain and in control. You just can't be, not if you are following God's plan for your life. It's time to let go.

Spend some time today meditating on this and deciding whether you are ready to accept the fact that you don't know it all, and that you can't know it all.

WEEK 1, DAY 7 – Galatians 3:1–6

We humans are foolish creatures, and we have extremely short-term memories. Throughout the Bible, this tendency plays out. God's people, even after seeing miracle upon miracle, so quickly forget what God has done and question whether He can help them in their current crisis. We all do this. We see the challenge in the path ahead, and we draw back. We worry. We question God. We doubt His ability to deliver us.

In this passage, you'll see a question something like this: *How can you not obey and believe after what you've seen God do?* One reason we find ourselves in this position is that we never spend adequate time thanking God for past miracles and keeping them at the top of our mind.

Your assignment for today: Make a list of five miracles in your life that are from God. As you move into Week 2, I want you to take a moment to thank God for one miracle or answered prayer or blessing each day and then meditate on it for a moment. Once you embrace what God has already done for you, it will make it far easier to believe He will guide you forward.

WEEK 2, DAY 1 – John 6:33

The God you serve has overcome the world. The God who raised Jesus from the grave is the same God who lives within you. The world holds no power over you. No one and nothing can interrupt God's promise and provision for you. Internalize this fundamental truth.

This week's meditations will focus on the pursuit of finding peace this week, but first, simply meditate on the truth that God is bigger than you, me, us, and whatever problems we are facing. If we don't believe that, we don't know God. If we do believe that, it's not rational for us to fear anything the world brings our way.

WEEK 2, DAY 2 – 2 Timothy 1:7

Most of us want peace. Most of us live in fear instead. Whether it's a relationship, your finances, a sin you've committed, a health issue, or your kids, fear can take over any given day. It can run your life. And it can ruin you in the process.

Here's the thing. Fear is not from God. He didn't design us that way. He gives us a spirit of power and love and a sound mind. When fear raises its ugly head in your life, that's a sign that something is not right between you and your God.

The next time you experience fear, take a closer look. Ask yourself what is driving this emotion. Where is this coming from? What's behind it? Look for the roots of it. And ask yourself, *What am I really afraid of?*

Finally, be on the lookout for fear disguised as another emotion. Much of our anger, for example, is just fear at its core. In many cases, our most regrettable character traits or specific actions are fueled in some way by fear.

WEEK 2, DAY 3 – Luke 12:27–34

This passage suggests that one of the reasons we find peace so elusive is that we need a new perspective. We're focusing on the trees, not the forest. These verses tell us not to worry about what we will eat or drink. Focus on seeking God, and everything else will fall into place. It's so hard to have real struggles, real worries, real problems sitting right in front of us and then push them to the side to look for God first.

If you really are unsure of where the next paycheck is coming from, or whether your marriage can be saved, or whether your loved one is going to survive surgery, it is easy to understand why trees would trump the forest. But that's not what we're called to do. And in the midst of real crises, we also consistently focus on smaller worries of what might or might not happen, at the expense of focusing on the plan God has for us.

If you wake up every day with a stomach ulcer or fall asleep every night fighting anxiety, it's likely that your eyes are currently set on the problem, and not the solution.

WEEK 2, DAY 4 – John 3:20–21

We all have things we're ashamed of, regrets from our past, sin that has overcome us, idols that have stood between us and our God. How in the world do we unwind all that? How in the world do we start living like we were intended to live?

Simply by stepping into the light.

In the shadows, in the darkness, the lies and the sins and the secrets win. They trap us. They steal our joy. They pull us farther from God and away from His promises. But as soon as we step into the light—walk with integrity, speak truth—all that begins to lose its grip. In Psalm 16, it says to trust Him, put Him in front, and follow the path. That path starts with a step out of the shadows, and it ends with joy, fulfillment, and pleasure like we've never experienced. The promise is real. Do you believe that?

WEEK 2, DAY 5 – Romans 9:20

Acceptance is critical to finding peace. Don't ask God why He made you the way you are. But if you feel you must ask, at least be willing to accept His answer. Most of us have trouble accepting ourselves and our lives. But how can we be at peace if we don't allow God to work in His own way? Our strengths, our weaknesses, everything is ordered, designed, and specifically intentioned to further His kingdom. Accept the good and the bad.

That includes your wounds—the experiences that have cut you the most deeply. The most violent, devastating traumas you have encountered. The harshest hurts. Your wounds are what will make you useful for God. You must accept and embrace them.

Think about this question. What is your greatest wound? And once you have a clear picture of it in your mind, accept it as part of your story. And then ask God why He gifted this hurt to you and how He would have you use it for His glory.

WEEK 2, DAY 6 – Ephesians 4:17–25

Wake up! Walk differently! This is the way to peace and ultimately joy. Too often, we self-medicate and numb ourselves to deal with pain. We give up on finding true peace and substitute with dangerous, short-lived, and unsuccessful attempts to cover the pain so we don't feel it any longer. This passage calls you to walk differently from those who are blind and ignorant, who are numb and beyond feelings, because you have been called to be a new person.

Spend today's quiet time focused on waking yourself up. Shaking yourself out of the trance. Freeing yourself from the fog and haze of whatever it is you've been using to medicate your pain and suffering. Let yourself feel it. No matter what it is or how much it hurts. Be present. Actually engage with your life. That's where healing will start. That's where the road to peace will begin. Stop numbing yourself. Stop wandering through your day in a zombie-like state. Dial it in. Wake it up. And let's start walking differently!

WEEK 2, DAY 7 – Ephesians 4:31–32

Tough request for you today. Think of someone in your life who has hurt you badly. Someone who has betrayed you in ways that are unimaginable. Think about the cruelest, most damaging thing that has ever happened to you, and then call up the face of the person responsible for it. Do you have a clear picture in your mind?

Now, I want you to let it go. Forgive that person. Release the resentment you've carried for far too long. Give it up to God. Stop carrying the burden of it. Be free.

And once you've done that, follow this exercise with anyone else in your life who has wronged you in any meaningful way (by this I mean anyone who has created resentment in your heart).

Resentment is cancer. It is a parasite that will steal peace from you and rob you of happiness. It will color the world around you and the soul within you. You will be a shadow of who you were designed to be. You have to let it go. I know it's not easy. It hasn't been easy for me. But it is required if you truly want to be at peace. Resentment allows the hurts of the past to continue to hurt us in the future.

Now the flip side of this coin is considering who might be harboring resentment because of you. Who do you need to make amends with in your life? That list of people is just as important to address as the list of those who have harmed you. Experiencing peace is about extending forgiveness to those who have hurt us and sincerely asking forgiveness of those we have harmed.

WEEK 3, DAY 1 – Hebrews 13:5

Be content. If you can accomplish this, you will have traveled far closer to God. In our society and culture, we're trained to never be satisfied. We consume. We produce. We perform. We compete. We climb ladders and mountains. We run marathons. We collect stuff. And we never fill the hole inside us. Let me ask you a question. What if you were to live today as if you were one of the lucky ones? You know, someone who had been given a second chance. Someone who had survived cancer or come back from a personal tragedy. What if you were just happy to be here? What would that feel like?

You have a God who has saved you, who says He will never leave you or forsake you. A God who has prepared treasures for you in heaven. You are one of the lucky ones. You are fortunate to be here. You already are living in your second chance. God has provided for you specifically according to His will. That might mean you don't have the success, possessions, or talents that you notice in others. But you already have everything you need. Anything else is an extra gift, a cherry on top.

Stop for a moment today and truly internalize what God has done for you. Not the way you go through the motions with the Lord's Supper at church. Rest in the fact that you are lucky. And that you've been blessed. Stop with the endless expectations. They will make every day a failure. You will always fall short of the world's yardstick.

God has shared His ultimate gift with you. And he's also provided you with special talents, experiences, and trials—and all of them make you a uniquely powerful human being. Explore how this is true for you instead of chasing the fleeting satisfactions of the world we live in.

WEEK 3, DAY 2 – Galatians 5:1, 2 Corinthians 5:17

Why did God set us free? It's not a trick question. The answer is so we might experience freedom. We've been made new. Not so we can be burdened, chained, and enslaved by something else. Far too often, we fall right back into slavery. If you obey anything other than God, you will be a slave to it.

It will capture you. Incarcerate you. Steal your joy.

Question: What has you in a cage? Call out the specific sin, addiction, idol, or obstacle that has you shackled and chained. This is the first step to unlocking joy.

WEEK 3, DAY 3 – Ephesians 6:12

You are a liar. And the person you've lied to the most is yourself. Over the course of our lives, we all develop negative internal beliefs that, left unchecked, have enormous power in defining who we are and how we feel about ourselves. These lies create a laundry list of unfortunate outcomes, ranging from doubt to depression to self-destruction. And over time, they just get stronger and stronger until they have strangled any truth we can see about the person God designed us to be.

These lies, of course, are not of God. They come entirely from somewhere else. This passage says that our struggles are not against flesh and blood but against powers and dark forces of wickedness. Satan, in other words. I wake up every day prepared for the lies that will come my way. For a long time, I just bought into those lies. Those voices in my head that told me I was less than, not enough, unclean, unworthy. Those voices that told me I would be abandoned, or that I would never measure up. Not everyone hears the same lies, but we all hear lies of some kind. The first step in taking away their power is to identify them.

So what is the biggest lie, the most self-defeating internal belief that you have about yourself? Really spend some time defining it, writing it down on paper, examining it. It's time to start taking away its power in your life.

WEEK 3, DAY 4 – Galatians 6:2

We are called to support one another, to bear each other's burdens, to hold each other accountable. Status quo for most men is to go lone wolf instead. To have acquaintances and "friends," but no real accountability or support. As a result, we can feel alone in a crowd, isolated in the midst of a sea of people. We must know and be known by others to truly experience God and the joy He has for us.

Your assignment: Make a list of three people in your life you can go deep with. Choose carefully, because you need to have enough faith and trust in these people to share your struggles, to let them know all of you and not just the superficial stuff.

When you are ready, I'd encourage you to meet with each of these people individually, share where you are on your journey, and ask them if they will walk with you. It will be the best action you've ever taken. I promise there are individuals in your life just waiting for you to ask them.

WEEK 3, DAY 5 – Psalm 107

We have all burdened the Lord with prayers. But how often do we praise Him? How often do we thank Him? How often do we truly sit in appreciation of what He's done in our lives?

Today, take a few moments to be thankful. Start your prayer time with thanksgiving instead of a punch list of your greatest needs. There is joy to be found in thanksgiving. It takes us out of self-serve mode and helps us see that we truly are fortunate and have been blessed beyond measure already.

WEEK 3, DAY 6 – Joshua 1:15, Luke 14:11–14

You've heard it before. The best way to help yourself is to help others. Service is an extremely powerful way to find joy. In these passages, you see a blueprint for what this should look like, including the fact that you should help others first (before expecting your own joy) and that your focus should be on helping those who can do nothing for you in return.

We are all very familiar with trading favors, or you-scratch-my-back-and-I'll-scratch-yours bargaining. We are masters at managing relationships to eventually get what we need from the other person. Not in a manipulative way, necessarily, but the tendency is to give with at least a subconscious expectation of what we might get in return.

True giving occurs when we are fairly certain there's no reciprocation coming our way. Think about how you can truly bless others in your life, especially those who aren't likely to pay you back. That could mean underprivileged people, of course. But it could also mean anonymous acts of kindness or blessing your enemies, among other things.

WEEK 3, DAY 7 – 1 Peter 4:12–16, Job 5:17

Two big ideas for today. First, we should rejoice in suffering. We shouldn't see it as strange when we endure a fiery trial. Actually, if we have God within us, we will experience trials and tribulations. The reasons for trauma, affliction, or however you want to define it are many. It helps strengthen our faith. It helps us empathize with others. It helps us see what God has done for us. The list goes on. But the bottom line is this. It says "if anyone suffers as a Christian, let him not be ashamed, but let him glorify God in this matter" (1 Pet. 4:16).

Second, there's another potential reason that affliction is showing up in your life. It may be that you are being disciplined. Our sin, our addictions, our idols all create consequences. And those consequences can be painful.

Job says "happy is the man that God corrects." In God's loving correction and in the pain of our consequences in sin, we can experience growth and strength. Just like a child who is disciplined by a parent. We can learn a lesson. We can learn from mistakes. We can grow closer to God as a result of those mistakes.

What is God correcting in your life at the moment? What is the point of any difficulties that are present in your life? What does God want you to learn? Approach this with eagerness, because joy awaits in the answers.

Notes

Introduction

1. Richard Rohr, *Breathing Under Water: Spirituality and the Twelve Steps* (Cincinnati: St. Anthony Messenger Press, 2011), 5.

Chapter 3

1. Robert Macfarlane, *Mountains of the Mind: Adventures in Reaching the Summit* (New York: Vintage Books, 2003), 18.

Chapter 4

1. Steve Sussman, Nadra Lisha, and Mark Griffiths, "Prevalence of the Addictions: A Problem of the Majority or the Minority?" *Evaluation & the Health Professions* 35, no. 1 (March 2011): 3–56, https://www .ncbi.nlm.nih.gov/pmc/articles/PMC3134413/.

2. "Overweight & Obesity Statistics," *National Institute of Diabetes and Digestive and Kidney Diseases*, https://www.niddk.nih.gov/health-information /health-statistics/overweight-obesity.

3. S.R. Dube, R.F. Anda, et al., "Long-Term Consequences of Childhood Sexual Abuse by Gender of Victim," *American Journal of Preventative Medicine* 28 (2005): 430–438.

4. Patricia Tjaden, and Nancy Thoennes. "Prevalence, Incidence, and Consequences of Violence Against Women: Findings from the National Violence Against Women Survey," *National Institute of Justice, Centers for Disease Control and Prevention* (November 1998), https://www.ncjrs .gov/pdffiles/172837.pdf.

5. "Addiction Medicine: Closing the Gap between Science and Practice," *The National Center on Addiction and Substance Abuse* (June 2012), https://www.centeronaddiction.org/sites/default/files/Addiction-medicine-closing-the-gap-between-science-and-practice_1.pdf.

6. Josh Katz, "Drug Deaths in America Are Rising Faster Than Ever," *The New York Times*, June 5, 2017, at https://www.nytimes.com/interactive/2017/06/05/upshot/opioid-epidemic-drug-overdose-deaths-are-rising-faster-than-ever.html.

7. "Suicide Facts," *SAVE*, https://save.org/about-suicide/suicide-facts/.

8. Andrew M. Weisberg, "The Cost of Keeping Prostitution Illegal," *Moneycation*, March 6, 2014, http://www.moneycation.com/2014/03/the-cost-of-keeping-prostitution-illegal.html?m=1.

9. "New Survey of Porn Use: Men and Women Watching in Startling Numbers," *Church Militant* (January 18, 216), https://www.churchmilitant.com/news/article/new-survey-of-porn-use-shows-startling-stats-for-men-and-women.

10. "Trends & Statistics," *National Institutes of Health* (April 2017), https://www.drugabuse.gov/related-topics/trends-statistics.

11. "The Prison Crisis," *American Civil Liberties Union* (January 20, 2011), https://www.aclu.org/prison-crisis.

12. "Pain Raises Risk of Opioid Addiction," *HealthDay*, https://consumer.healthday.com/bone-and-joint-information-4/pain-health-news-520/pain-raises-risk-of-opioid-addiction-713140.html.

13. "About the CDC-Kaiser ACE Study," *Centers for Disease Control and Prevention*, https://www.cdc.gov/violenceprevention/acestudy/about.html.

14. Johann Hari, *Chasing the Scream: The First and Last Days of the War on Drugs* (New York: Bloomsbury USA, 2015).

15. Edmund Burke, *A Philosophical Enquiry into the Origin of Our Ideas of the Sublime and Beautiful*, Ed. A. Philips (Oxford: Oxford University Press, 1990), https://sites.google.com/site/kunstfilosofiesite/Home/texts/burke-on-the-sublime.

16. Alexander MacLaren, *MacLaren's Commentary: Expositions of Holy Scripture* (Harrington, DE: Delmarva Publications, 2013), *Bible Hub*, http://biblehub.com/commentaries/maclaren/psalms/63.htm.

17. Johann Hari, 293.

18. David M. Kolker, "Drug and Alcohol Rehabilitation Continued to Fail: How Many Kids Must Die before We Change?" *Psych Central*, https://psychcentral.com/blog/drug-and-alcohol-rehabilitation-continues-to-fail-how-many-kids-must-die-before-we-change/.

Chapter 6

1. Toni Morrison, *Beloved* (New York: Vintage Books, 1987), 88.

Chapter 14

1. Tan Hecheng, *The Killing Wind: A Chinese County's Descent into Madness during the Cultural Revolution* (New York: Oxford University Press, 2017).

Chapter 18

1. MacLaren, *MacLaren's Commentary*.

2. Ibid.

Chapter 21

1. Erika Hayasaki, "End Pain Forever: How a Single Gene Could Become a Volume Knob for Human Suffering," *Wired*, April 18, 2017, https://www.wired.com/2017/04/the-cure-for-pain/.

2. Mike Wilkerson, *Redemption: Freed by Jesus from the Idols We Worship and the Wounds We Carry* (Wheaton, IL: Crossway, 2011), 37.

3. Ibid.

4. "The Backwards Brain Bicycle," *YouTube*, https://www.youtube.com/watch?v=MFzDaBzBlL0.

5. "Navy Seal Commander Gives Some of the Best Advice to Grads at Commencement," *YouTube*, https://youtu.be/K13p1DlsDMQ.

Chapter 24

1. Dan B. Allender, *To Be Told: Know Your Story, Shape Your Future* (Colorado Springs, CO: Waterbrook Press, 2011), 47–53.
2. Ibid., 116.
3. Ibid., 117.
4. Timothy D. Wilson, *Strangers to Ourselves: Discovering the Adaptive Unconscious* (Cambridge, MA: Harvard University Press, 2002).
5. Anne Lamott, *Stitches: A Handbook on Meaning, Hope and Repair* (New York: Riverhead Books, 2013), 93.
6. Malcolm Owen Slavin and Daniel Kriegman, *The Adaptive Design of the Human Psyche*, quoted in John Bradshaw, *Healing the Shame That Binds You* (Deerfield Beach, FL: Health Communications, 2005), 278.

Chapter 25

1. "The Curse of the Bradford Pear," *USA Today*, https://www.usatoday.com/story/news/nation-now/2016/03/30/curse-bradford-pear-column/82416560/.

Chapter 28

1. Melody Beattie, *Codependent No More* (Center City, MN: Hazelden Publishing, 1992), 146.
2. Robert J. Morgan, *Reclaiming the Lost Art of Biblical Meditation* (Nashville: Thomas Nelson, 2017), 78.

Chapter 30

1. David Foster Wallace, *This Is Water: Some Thoughts, Delivered on a Significant Occasion about Living a Compassionate Life* (New York: Little, Brown and Company, 2009), 120.

Tools & Resources

1. Mike Wilkerson, *Redemption*, 66.

Notes

2. Patrick Carnes, *Out of the Shadows: Understanding Sexual Addiction* (Center City, MN: Hazelden Publishing, 2001).
3. Mark R. Laaser, *Healing the Wounds of Sexual Addiction* (Grand Rapids, MI: Zondervan, 2004).

www.ingramcontent.com/pod-product-compliance
Lightning Source LLC
Chambersburg PA
CBHW062059080426
42734CB00012B/2696